MW01172703

PLANTING SEEDS IN A CONCRETE JUNGLE

KEVIN ASHER

Copyright 2024 Kevin Asher. All rights reserved

Special thanks to Jean Asher and Imani Asher for their help with editing.

ISBN: 979-8-9909361-2-6

INTRODUCTION

Planting Seeds in a Concrete Jungle is a collection of personal stories written and illustrated by Dr Kevin Asher. It is an inspiring, easy to read account of the author's journey from Kingston, Jamaica, to the cold, harsh reality of life in the ghettos of the USA. Set during the turbulent millennial years (1980-2000,) we are taken on a ride from Kingston, Jamaica, to the concrete jungles of Washington, DC - from a third world capital to a first world metropolis that was reeling from the devastating impact of a crack-cocaine epidemic. It is a journey that takes us from impressionable teenager, through the responsibilities of fatherhood, and the five children who came along for the ride.

Told via 15 independent short stories and a number of poems/essays, we follow the transformation of a young naïve Black male, new to the USA, who is forced to adapt and assimilate, without becoming a victim of his stereotype and yielding to the temptations of crime and drugs. The book is full of important life lessons on manifesting your dreams, maintaining your focus, and thriving in any environment. Relying on the age-old teachings from his mother, we are introduced to a mindset that can keep one grounded, goal oriented, and humble during their formative years.

By breaking the main story into several short stories/poems/essays, The over 200 pages become less intimidating. Readers can read a story or poem and walk away feeling they have accomplished something meaningful for their efforts. The creative storytelling and unique perspective of the author will bring readers back for more (and more.) The content and quality of the book will make it attractive to even the most seasoned readers.

Planting Seeds in a Concrete Jungle guarantees to be a delightful read, infused with humor, important historical events, Jamaican *patois*, and some very thought-provoking poetry. It is a refreshing reminder of how self-belief, hard work and discipline can help one grow and thrive anywhere. Even if your seed was planted in a concrete jungle.

CONTENTS

SHORT STORIES

SUBSTANCE OVER HYPE

"Showoff brings disgrace"

It was an early Jamaican Saturday morning when most kids were finishing their chores. I had just completed raking the leaves from our front yard. There was a patch of dirt right next to the front of our house that looked like a hardened mini sand pit; much like the one used by long jumpers; devoid of leaves, it looked as inviting as a just raked one. Furthermore, the area was under a huge mango tree, which provided shade from the sun and made that plot of land the perfect site for our weekend marble games.

That day, my friend and opponent would be Dervin. It was the winner take all match. We each brought a one-quart plastic bucket, filled with marbles, to the match. Win or lose, it was going to be a long day and as usual, I was in it to win it.

The game was taking place right under the window of my mother's bedroom. Dervin was down to his last two marbles, and I heard cheers (from my mother and younger brother, Keith). I was about to destroy Dervin - but the cheers were not only getting louder, but they're also not meant for me, the kindred son. They were for Dervin!

To give some background: my mother had eight children, listed here in descending order of age: Jennifer, Jean, Maurice, Milton, Jackie, Karen, and bringing up the rear were me and my youngest brother, Keith.

I always felt that my mother (mama) was a good mother. There was always food on the table and a roof over our heads. She taught us values, manners, and respect for others. Our father was rarely around, so from my perspective, my mother did virtually all the parental heavy lifting.

Once, when I got on the commuter bus without paying my fare, she marched me right back to the conductor and made me pay for it. If I dared to pass any of my elderly neighbors without saying "good morning " or "good evening," I would be disciplined by my mama.

By the time Keith and I became teenagers, mama was a seasoned parent. Discipline was her modus operandi. We could not leave the house after we got home from school on weekdays, and we had to be home before dark on the weekends. She regulated who came to our house and the homes we could visit. School work and homework were the priority during the week, and chores were a must on the weekends. I rebelled against all the above and butted heads with my mama constantly. I probably spent more time and energy trying to avoid doing chores than it took to complete them. After all, she was restricting our freedoms, and somebody had to resist. A significant part of my childhood was devoted to devising new means to skirt those restrictions.

For me, staying at home, without friends, was akin to solitary confinement. I was constantly on the move, and socializing outside of the home was always on my agenda. I was also extremely competitive and took naturally to sports. I was the only one in my family who played a sport of any kind.

My younger brother, Keith, was more interested in reading than sports. He was not at all competitive either. Whenever we played together, I usually won, and I rubbed it in. It was not enough to just win, by the way, I had to brag and boast to complete the victory. Keith had a short temper, and I knew how to press his temper button.

Invariably, our games ended with us fighting. On the grounds of being older, I was the one held responsible for those fights.

Keith, deservedly, got most of the attention from my parents. He was very asthmatic, so mama was always caring for him. He also spent a lot of time traveling the country with my father, who traveled a lot when he worked. To me, there was nothing more boring and nausea inducing than sitting in a car or bus, doing nothing for hours. So, I did not make any of those trips.

I liked to spend my leisure time in action mode. This could mean sneaking out to play football at the park or ping pong at my best friend Glen's house. If I'm being honest, I was never a gracious winner in any of the aforementioned activities and spent a lot of my time cultivating a fan-base dying to see me lose. Which brings me back to my marble game, in my front yard, under my mother's bedroom window…

Recap: Dervin was losing big time. He is down to his last two marbles. His shooting marble had rolled a few inches from mine after his last shot. All I had to do now was hit his marble with mine (worth two marbles) and the game would be over.

Was I using the occasion to brag and show off? Hell yes! It was how I rolled (no pun intended.) Not only did I promise to kill his marble, but I was also going to offer it as a sacrifice to the marble gods!

The cheering had now quieted. Suddenly, the birds stopped chirping and the dogs stopped barking. Silence. Everyone watching the game was frozen in suspended animation, awaiting the outcome of my next move.

I looked up and saw mama had retreated somewhat, from the window into the shadows of her room. She knew that the game would be over in a few seconds, but she was still eying my next shot. Dervin's marble was so close to mine that Stevie Wonder could make the shot.

While I was accustomed to competing with spectators and even friends, cheering against me, this was the first time that someone from my family, let alone my mother, was among the "Boo Birds."

It is quite natural for people to root for the underdog. A competition is not a competition without competition. If one person is always winning, then the game gets predictable and boring. I got that. But mama?

Reflecting back, I can appreciate the differences in our game. Dervin was the underdog; he had an awkward way of gripping the marble; he left his forefinger sticking straight out and nobody else did that.

Though the odds were steep, Dervin had proven to be a formidable and gracious opponent. It was back and forth for roughly two hours. He complimented me when I made difficult shots, and with me on the verge of victory, Dervin was congratulating me already. He displayed many of the qualities that mama was trying to instill in her kids: modesty, humility, respect, and graciousness, and my mother was right there in his corner.

I, on the other hand, was tooting my horn the entire game. I laughed at his missed shots and teased his awkward grip on the marble. I might have even bragged about world domination in marbles. I was in the trash talk zone, so my mouth was on autopilot. Victory was a chip shot away. My mother and brother were there as witnesses. What more could I ask for?

I missed the shot. Yes, I missed the (expletive deleted) shot. Still cannot explain it to this day. My poise and confidence went AWOL and never returned, after that miss.

Dervin sprung back to life and took advantage of my mental collapse and proceeded to pick off my marbles one by one. When he took the last marble from my bucket, Dervin cracked his first smile of the morning.

It was a humbling experience. I had lost all my marbles, literally and figuratively.

I looked up at the window to see mama nodding approvingly as she retreated further into the shadows of her room.

"*Showoff brings disgrace,*" an old Jamaican rebuke, was what I would hear from her in moments like this. I could hear her thinking it and it was reverberating in my ears at that moment.

Interestingly, mama never mentioned a word about the loss to me. She did not have to. Her point was made, loud and clear. Unlike some other people, she found no joy in dancing on anyone's grave.

I learned an important lesson: respect your opponent and save the celebration until after the game is over. Always bring substance, not hype, to your performances and remember, "showoff brings disgrace."

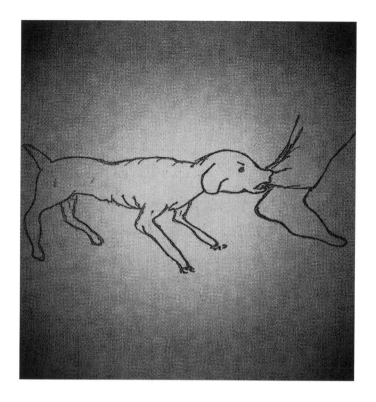

CASTING PEARLS BEFORE MONGRELS

"Sorry fi mawga dog, mawga dog tun roun bite yuh"

Mongrel, or mutt dogs, are a fixture across Jamaica's landscape. They are the stray, unclaimed, feral dogs that you will see roaming the streets and alleys of the country. No collars, no tags, no microchip, no love.

Mongrels are usually emaciated, or mawga, as Jamaicans prefer to say, and are experts at survival. They are everywhere – on the streets, in the parks, and as uninvited guests in your yard. One even managed to make it on to the soccer field at the national stadium, during an internationally televised game. Not even the dozens of match security stewards or the police could get this dog off the field. He ended up being on the field for the duration of the second half of that game, skillfully avoiding the players, match officials and match security. I think that they should take the alligator off Jamaica's Coat of Arms and replace it with a mongrel dog.

Mongrels are so ubiquitous that eventually, one or more will find their way into your heart and your home. Just about every yard in Jamaica will have two or three of them, if for nothing more than security. They bark and alert you when someone approaches or enters your yard and in exchange, you feed them the scraps from your table. They do not come into the house. It is understood that they sleep outside under the trees or the eaves of the roof. It is a very formal, symbiotic, and healthy relationship that changes, however, when mating season comes around. Then, primal animal instincts prevail and ultimately upset this established order.

Jamaica as a country, has not evolved to the point where animal welfare is on the front page of public policy. Yes, we all know that you should treat animals with respect and compassion, and there are consequences for doing otherwise. Neutering and spaying, though, the best cure for unwanted dogs, remains in the domain of the upper class. Jamaica does not have the resources, the infrastructure, or the will to spay and neuter these stray dogs. The best most people will do is to try and lock their dogs away until the animals are no longer in heat. That is often a long shot, though. Dogs will be dogs, and nothing stands between two dogs in heat.

Once, for example, I locked away our female dog, Blackie, in the house during mating season. I checked every door and window before leaving the house, to make sure that they were locked securely. When we returned home that night, my dog was hitched to a male dog in the living room. How that male dog got into the house is still a mystery. There was nothing missing from the house, so I guess that no burglars were involved. Seems to me, the burglars could learn a thing or two from these dogs in heat.

In any case, the mongrels grow in numbers after each mating season, and they become a nuisance. They chase cars and people and spill your trash all over the sidewalks. We had two mongrels in our yard when I was entering my teenage years. With one being a female (Blackie), it meant puppies were on the horizon next mating season.

It came as a huge surprise then, when my younger brother, Keith, brought home a puppy and took it straight into the house. It was another mongrel. Not the typical mongrel, though. This one had long, black, shiny hair and a pointed mouth. Unlike the short, tan/brown hair and rounded mouth of the typical mongrel. Keith's puppy looked like it had some pedigree so, this dog was allowed in the house and slept on the front verandah. Keith named the puppy "Uncas." Do not ask me where he got that name from. It was his dog and I never asked.

After a couple months with us, Uncas was mature enough to become afflicted by the bacchanalian debauchery called mating season. We could not prevent Uncas from leaving our yard and looking for mates. When we locked the front gate, he would finesse his way through the barbed wire/ thorny bush fence that separated us from our neighbors. To find a mating partner, there were no "dog seeking dog" ads on Dogslist or an Ashley Madison canine edition. It was strictly animal instincts - see dog of opposite sex, mate dog of opposite sex. The survival of the species is their ultimate goal, and trust me, all dogs are passionately on board with this policy.

On one of these pheromone-induced escapades, Uncas got a deep laceration from the barbed wire he was trying to finesse, over the knee of his hind leg. Our best efforts at wound care were proving futile, as the wound became infected and contaminated with maggots.

In our home, I had seen many dogs come and go, in my short lifetime. Even had to bury a few in the backyard myself. Whenever our dogs got sick, our options for treatment were limited. For intestinal issues, we gave our dogs a brown liquid called "lamp oil" to drink. Their cuts and bites were dressed using a lavender liquid known as "Jaye's liquid." That was all we had to offer our ailing dogs. If these failed, with due compassion and respect, the shovel was next.

This was Uncas though, Keith's dog. For the first and only time I can remember, we decided to take a dog to the animal hospital. The only animal hospital we knew at the time was in Trench Town, arguably the toughest neighborhood in Jamaica, as far as crime and violence were concerned. That was why we never, ever thought about taking a dog there before, let alone a mongrel. Again, this was Uncas.

The next Saturday morning we got up early and prepared for our trip to the animal hospital. Mama made me accompany Keith. We were expecting the usual Saturday morning shopping crowd on the buses, so we planned on getting there early. I had gotten a cardboard box to carry Uncas in. By now, he was unable to walk. About five months old at the time, and weighing almost twenty pounds, he could barely fit in the box. We had to leave the top open for him to fit.

We got our bus fares from mama, and off we went. Keith and I got on the bus and were somewhat surprised that so few people were on the bus. The bus dropped us off right in front of the hospital. Again, no crowd. Trench Town, it seemed, was still asleep. "Closed until further notice," the sign pasted on the front door read. Just our luck!

"Back home again, with poor Uncas," I thought, as we crossed the road to catch the bus home. By this time, however, Jamaica had awakened. The buses that stopped were way too crowded to fit me, Keith, and a dog. In fact, some of the bus conductors refused to allow the dog on the bus:

"Yu can't come on MY bus with dat dog," a conductor stated in no uncertain manner. By the look on his face you would think that I disrespected his mother.

Passengers also chimed in to voice their opposition: " Me no pay my bus fare to sit down beside no dog. Don't bring yu dog on the bus!"

At 13 years old, I was not old enough to challenge any of those adults.

The buses are usually very crowded on Saturdays. It is the day when most people do their grocery shopping and get fresh fruits and vegetables from the market. Coronation Market, the largest produce market in Jamaica, is less than a mile from the animal hospital. Pedestrian and vehicular traffic in the area are always very heavy on Saturdays. It is shoulder to shoulder on the sidewalks and bumper to bumper on the road.

By now it was just after midday, the bus stop offered no shelter from the sun, and it seemed that all the buses for this route home had refused to allow us onboard. We had some serious decisions to make with the day drifting by. We could walk to the bus terminus, about half a mile away, where the buses start off empty, or we could just make the two mile walk home.

Being the lazy one, I convinced Keith that we should carry Uncas to the bus terminus and take our chances there. As the older, bigger sibling, I carried Uncas. What a spectacle: two, light skinned, "red" boys, likely from uptown, carrying a dog amongst a sea of dark-skinned pedestrians, downtown. Boy did we get stared at in a "WTF" kind of way.

Ignoring the stares and snickers, we inched our way along until we reached the crowded terminus. Here again, none of the buses would allow us on with the dog. Now, Keith and I were looking at the prospects of a three mile walk home carrying an ailing dog. It was hot, we were tired and hungry, but we had to get moving. Sundown was fast approaching, and our route home would take us back past Trench Town. Not even mongrel dogs are out after dark in Trench Town.

It was a different walk back home. The sun seemed hotter, the dog heavier and our patience thinner. Uncas was also getting restless in the box. His shifting weight made him more difficult to carry. It is worth mentioning again, we (Keith, Uncas, and I) were all hungry and exhausted.

By the time we passed Collie Smith Drive (the entrance to Trench Town,) Keith and I were busted. The cardboard box was falling apart, and my hands gave up.

"Mi can't carry this dog no more." I said to Keith, who nodded his empathy for my plight. He could not handle the job either. I sat the box on the sidewalk. From there the choice was Uncas':

"If you want to go home, you have to walk," I said to Uncas.

We walked two paces ahead and motioned to Uncas to join us. Reluctantly, he emerged from the cardboard box and joined us for the walk home. He too recognized that Trench Town was no place to be after dark.

Uncas was limping at first, but soon was in full stride, walking with us the rest of the way home. From that moment on, with Jayes dressings, his wound got better, until it healed. No animal hospital required.

So complete was the healing that when mating season rolled around again, Uncas was up to his old tricks. He took off in search of fun and pheromones, never to be seen by again. He never returned home. Our efforts to find him all ended in vain.

Jamaicans have an old saying: "*Sorry fi mawga dog, mawga dog tun 'round bite yu.*" A mawga dog being a metaphor for someone without scruples or loyalty. Kindness to a mawga dog does not guarantee their loyalty or kindness in return. In our case, our mawga dog simply ran away!

Keith was devastated.

The Uncas experience taught some important lessons, though. Often, the best help you can give someone is to let them stand on their own feet. We get to our desired destinations best by putting one foot in front of the other. We may start off with uncertainty, but we usually hit full stride, with confidence, as our journey progresses. Lastly, for all the good and sacrifice you do on behalf of others, do not expect any thanks or loyalty in return. I will close with a quote from The Bible:

"When you do your good works, let not thy left hand know what thy right hand doeth. That thy good works be in secret, and thy Father which seeth in secret Himself, shall reward thee openly." (Can I get an Amen!)

Our kindness and compassion are among the reasons that dogs are still man's best friends. Let your kindness and compassion continue to flow to all, but approach "mawga dogs" with caution. As illustrated by the story, a "bite" does not have to be physical to inflict pain.

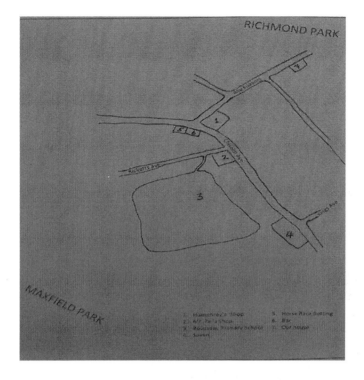

CHISHOLM AVENUE

"Show me your company and I will tell who you are"

Another Friday afternoon, classes are over and it is time for us children to head home from school. The weekend is officially here, and I am not looking forward to the chores and house work that lay-wait me on Saturday. I have decided to stay after school to play and hang out with classmates, so I can milk the last drops of fun we will have together until next Monday. My younger brother, Keith, has heeded the advice of our mother who wants us home immediately after school. Our school, Rousseau Primary, is located on Ricketts Avenue, where it meets Chisholm Avenue, and its proximity to Maxfield Park has always been a source of concern for my mother.

Rousseau's tall concrete perimeter wall, and a school full of teachers, make it a safe place to hang out with my friends to play without any worries. After a few hours of frolicking and sweat, I must head home before my mother returns from work.

Soon, we will confront the reality of class and economics lurking outside Rousseau's gates. Some of us will make a left turn, head down Ricketts Avenue towards Maxfield Park, a low-income community, while the rest of us will head in the opposite direction towards middle class Richmond Park. Before we can get to Richmond Park, however, we have to cross Chisholm Avenue.

As a child, I was intimidated by Chisholm Avenue. It was always busy with motor vehicle and pedestrian traffic that made getting from one side to the other difficult. Crossing was especially challenging during rush hours when a multitude of unaccompanied minors had to cross it to get to and from school. These were the days of no crossing guards, crosswalks, or stop signs. It was child versus wild!

Chisholm Avenue is also the unofficial boundary of the ghetto.

The postal service seemed to be aware of its boundary status when it assigned different postal codes to the communities on either side of Chisholm Avenue. On one side is Richmond Park, where I lived, with the postal code Kingston 10. It was a middle-class community that featured single family homes, neat lawns, and tidy streets. The further removed from Chisholm Avenue, the nicer the Richmond Park homes seemed. Our home on Queens Avenue was close to Chisholm Avenue, but a "Kingston10" house, nonetheless.

Meanwhile, on the other side of Chisholm Avenue, just at the corner, was Rousseau Primary, the elementary school I attended for five years. On that side, as you moved away from Chisholm Avenue, single family homes morphed into wooden/zinc shacks with increasing degree of dilapidation, until you were right smack in the community of Maxfield Park. This was ghetto central, with the assigned postal code, Kingston 13.

To recap: Richmond Park side of Chisholm Avenue - Kingston 10; the Rousseau Primary side – Kingston 13. One road dividing two communities, with two different postal codes.

There were two supermarkets where Queens Avenue met Chisholm Avenue. One on either side of the road. Both were "Chinese" owned. On the Richmond Park side was Humphrey's shop. His shop had an open layout where shoppers could enter the store, walk the aisles, grab the items for purchase and pay at the cash register close to the entrance. Across the street, on the "ghetto" side of Chisholm Avenue, was Mr. Tai's grocery shop, an off-track betting store, and a rum bar (the usual commercial trifecta of the ghetto.) I would have to really want a particular item from Mr. Tai's shop to go there, as it would mean that I would have two obstacles to overcome: first and foremost, I would have to cross the dreaded Chisholm Avenue. The other deterrent was the layout of Mr. Tai's shop. It was basically a storefront where burglar bars and plexiglass separated you from Mr. Tai, his assistants, and the goods. You gave them your order and they sourced your goods. If the shop was crowded, it became a shouting match to determine who got served. As a result, children were usually served last.

After I graduated from Rousseau Primary, our family fell on hard times. Mama had to downgrade from our Richmond Park home, and we moved into a rental home/tenement yard she owned at 7 Chisholm Avenue, Kingston 13 (affectionately referred to as "Seven.") Yes, on the ghetto side!

Mama inherited the property, with two run down houses on the lot, when grandma died. It became a major source of headaches. Mama was constantly chasing after tenants to collect rent, and it seemed that there was always something broken at Seven, in need of repairs. Keith and I were no fans of Seven either. We had to help with the paintings, cleanings, and repairs in between tenants.

By this time, mama had retired from her civil service job and the rents from Seven was her primary source of income. The rent payments, however, were inconsistent. I remember going with her to collect rent from a tenant and hearing the story about why they would not be able to pay their rent...for the tenth month in a row! (I thought mama was way too lenient with this tenant.) The tenants sometimes hid when they saw us approaching. Others would be asking when needed repairs would be addressed. Headache! Even for me, and it was not my house.

Mama partitioned one of the houses at Seven, after the previous occupants were evicted, and moved us in. Effectively making that house a duplex, with us occupying one half of the house. The idea behind the move, I would later find out, was so she could rent out the Richmond Park house. Since it was located in Kingston 10, mama could attract more reliable tenants, and charge a higher rent.

There were about six families living at Seven at the time, and I think a quick definition of a Jamaican "tenement yard " is warranted: Picture a single-family home with 'x' number of bedrooms, one bathroom, one kitchen, for example. Each bedroom is rented to a different person/family and they share the kitchen and bathroom. The close proximity in which the different families are forced to interact often creates friction and drama. Everyone knew everybody's business: you knew the times they got home; who was having problems with their mates, etc. Disagreements amongst the tenants, arguments, and sometimes fights were commonplace. Often, the tenants were not on speaking terms with each other as a result.

As mama's children, we could not get caught up in any of the squabbles and drama that were frequent. We also had to be respectful and polite to the tenants at all times. As such, we found it easier to keep to ourselves. Keith and I spent a lot of time playing on the front veranda.

That verandah was also our window seat to a bustling thoroughfare, Chisholm Avenue. With a parade of people passing by daily, I think I could identify everyone who lived within a five-mile radius of Seven. From that vantage point I have seen "grab-bag-men" snatch handbags from the arms of unsuspecting females. I've seen robbers get beaten by angry mobs. Witnessed a few motor vehicle accidents; and mostly watched ordinary people get on with their daily routines.

I remember one Saturday morning, about 5 a.m. I was sitting on the verandah with mama (we were both early risers) when two unknown young men jumped the gate and entered the front yard of Seven. They apparently did not see us. Mama, of course, took offence to their actions and was getting ready to chase them off her property. Just as she was about to confront the young men, she noticed one of them putting a gun into his waistband. Well, I did not know that my mother could moon-walk. She stealthily made her way back into the shadows of the verandah, where we watched and waited until the men jumped the back fence and headed towards Maxfield Park.

Inside the gates of Seven, I got to observe, human beings in the wild. Most were kind, decent people, trying to do better for themselves and their families. Occasionally, their ugly twin brothers/sisters would emerge.

A quiet, gentle young lady refused to speak to a soul at Seven for weeks because someone used her bath soap without her permission.

I never expected to hear a Bible toting, church going woman use words that belonged in the gutter...in front of her children, when asked why she left the bathroom so messy! I was not going to be the one to remind her of the old saying: "Cleanliness is next to Godliness." This cockroach was not going to partake in that fowl fight.

Another time, a tenant threw out his wife early one morning, because he was convinced she was having an affair. Nothing funny about that one.

And talk about gossip! Nothing was sacred or off limits. If the Dalai Lama were living at Seven, the tenants would be gossiping about him too:

Tenant A: "How come we never see him with a woman?"

Tenant B: "Is only man alone mi see him with. Yu right!"

Tenant A: "Yu thinking what I am thinking?"

Tenant A and B: "Ha, ha, ha, ha, ha, ha," both rolling on the ground.

By the time they finished with the Dalai, that perpetual smirk on his face would be replaced by a scowl.

For me, not much changed when we moved into Seven. My best friend, Glen, lived just across the street on Kings Avenue, in Richmond Park. Glen had a table tennis board and we always played there on the weekends. From my time at Rousseau Primary, I also knew most of the boys on the Seven side of the road.

Rousseau Primary, where I played football in the afternoons, was also right behind Seven. If I were up to the challenge, I would sometimes scale the big concrete wall in the backyard to get there.

On occasions, my love of soccer drew me to the gravel/dirt patch that doubled as a football field in heart of Maxfield Park. I couldn't let my mother know. She was under the impression that I was playing at Rousseau Primary with the boys from Richmond Park. Some of the best football in Jamaica was being played at Maxfield Park and I wanted to be part of that excitement. The passions were high, tackles were rough, and it was mostly fun.

Invariably fights broke out. Some of these fights could get violent. I remember one guy, they called him Scorcher, because of the fiery tackles he would inflict on us young ballers. He would brag afterwards, "if dem want to play big man football, dem haffi can tek big man tackle!" Not a single one of us youths cared much for Scorcher. He was built like Superman and used his size and reputation as a criminal gangster to intimidate us.

Once, after being on the business end of a hard tackle from a newcomer to the field, Scorcher retaliated, and a fist fight ensued. After they were separated, he ran to his house which was adjacent to the field. Scorcher re-emerged brandishing a gun, his friends in tow. They were desperately trying to restrain and convince him to calm down.

"Where yu going with dat?" His friends asked.

"Don't yu see him posse from Greenwich Farm? We don't want no trouble with dem gangsters." They said to Scorcher, pointing to a group of young men by the perimeter wall who looked like they were in full DEFCON Delta mode.

"Yu better go put down dat fool-fool revolver. Yu can't do nothing with dat!" one shouted. Eventually Scorcher calmed down and heeded their advice, averting a crisis. Naturally, the football game was over after that.

This was the first time I had been that close to an unholstered gun. I spent so much time staring at it that I am sure I would recognize that gun if I saw it again. My heart was pumping so hard and fast, I think my blood etched a replica of the gun in my brain.

Walking home that evening, my adrenalin level subsiding, I could now reflect on the events that transpired and how close to the edge we were. As I mused on the events that led to the scuffle, I could not help but chuckle to myself: a big man who couldn't "tek big man tackle."

That afternoon was the last time that I would play football at Maxfield Park.

The overwhelming majority of Maxfield Park residents were good, law-abiding citizens, but a few criminal/political gangs were known to operate in and around that area. Nightfall would certainly not catch me there. I have to say it again - my mother would kill me if she knew that I was there. As far as she was concerned, there were too many hoodlums there for her comfort, and she did not want any of her children to fall under their influence.

"*Show me your company and I will tell you who you are,*" she would say, time and time again, to warn us of the dangers of hanging out with people she did not approve of.

Within Maxfield Park, an outsider was granted a certain degree of immunity if he were a footballer. However, you still had to be weary of the threats from outside gangs and the police. Yes, the police! If you were caught on the streets of Maxfield Park after 11 pm, there was a good chance you would be beaten and/or arrested by the police. It was generally assumed that you were up to no good. The residents might even applaud the police for taking "troublemakers" off their streets. Those days, the police could take any and all kind of liberties with people from the ghetto, without any consequences. Sometimes the police could be worse than the gangsters. So, when the police jeep pulled up into that community at night, people scattered.

Returning home one evening after playing football at Rousseau Primary, I noticed a small crowd on Chisholm Avenue, outside Mr. Tai's shop. There was a muscular man, his face covered by a blood-soaked towel, lying lifeless on the sidewalk. He was hit by a car while running across Chisholm Avenue. The scene was gruesome. I did not have the strength to look at his bloody, mangled body, so I quickly turned my head and walked away.

"Another victim of Chisolm Avenue," I thought.

I then noticed a larger crowd of onlookers gathered directly in front of Humphrey's shop across the street. I hastily crossed Chisholm Avenue to investigate, and saw a young man, about 20 years old, lying face down, motionless, in a pool of blood on the dirt path we called a sidewalk. He was a few yards from Humphrey's entrance and was still alive.

According to eye witnesses, both men tried to rob Humphrey's shop a few minutes earlier. Humphrey shot one of the robbers and the other was fatally struck by a car as he fled across Chisholm Avenue. I thought I knew everyone from this part of town, but I did not recognize the guy lying on the ground in front of Humphrey's. I did, however, recognize the brown, rusty revolver with the black tape around the handle, a few inches from his hand. It was Scorcher's gun. It suddenly became clear to me that the man under the towel, on the other side of Chisolm Avenue was Scorcher. This realization left me conflicted. I should be feeling some type of empathy for someone in a fatal accident, but there was none. Scorcher was a serial offender who terrorized his neighborhood and loved to intimidate us youngsters. I don't think anybody would have wished him this terrible ending, but I doubted that many people were going to miss him.

My attention was captured by the young man laying prone in front of me.

It was hard to tell if he was dead or alive. There was no moaning, groaning, writhing, flailing or any signs of pain or agony. His eyes were closed and he seemed to be in suspended animation. Had it not been for the visible blood loss, you would think that he was resting. Except he was still breathing. I could tell because every time he inhaled or exhaled, the grains of sand adjacent to his nostril moved back and forth. A wave of anxiety and fear swept over me as I thought that he was going to die momentarily. At the same time, I was paralyzed by those emotions. "Why wasn't anybody trying to save him?" I thought.

This was my first time at a crime scene involving dead people, and dare I say, I did not know how to act. I pretended to be cool and feigned the indifference that was rampant within the crowd of onlookers. With all the adults around, this 14-year-old was not going to make the first move.

At that time, fear was the jockey galloping my heart. Even looking at the grains of sand moving next to the guy's nostrils was a trigger for anxiety. Every now and then there would be a stretch where no sand grains moved and I would think the worst had happened. Then they would start moving again - back and forth, like the pendulum of a clock, ticking down the final seconds.

"Anybody know dis boy?" A lady asked, to blank stares and shaking heads.

"First time mi see him," another added.

"Is whe Scorcha get him from?" the conversation continued before she was interrupted.

"Scorcha, get wha him deserve!" A man shouted to nodding approval all around.

The young man in front of Humphrey's shop seemed to deserve a different fate, though. His clothes were clean and ironed, and his hair neatly trimmed, suggesting he was from a good family. He even had a modest gold chain with a gold cross pendant around his neck.

"He shouldn't be here," I remembered thinking.

Nobody else in the crowd seemed to share my sentiments, however. The predominant feelings were scorn and condemnation for the two brazen, daylight robbers.

There was a spate of burglaries in and around Richmond Park during the previous months. The betting shop was robbed the week before, and Humphrey had been robbed at gunpoint, two months earlier. That was why Humphrey bought his gun, someone mentioned. Things were so bad that if anyone were caught stealing in the community, they would be guaranteed two beatings: one from angry locals eager to take out their frustrations via "mob justice," and another from the police who would "rescue" them from the mob.

"Anybody call di ambulance?" A voice from the crowd enquired, interrupting the monotony of indifference.

(Cell phones didn't exist then, and telephones were a luxury limited to a few homes in Richmond Park.)

"No! Mek dem call police," someone responded. "Police know how fi deal wid dem."

"Dem a thief! Dem fi dead!" A voice shouted.

A man then walked up to the dying young man on the ground and popped the gold chain from his neck. "Yu not going to need dis where yu going," he stated as he pocketed the chain. "Thief!" He said in disgust, as he walked off, overlooking the fact that he too, was now a thief.

After about 20 minutes of watching and waiting, the grains of sand adjacent to the nose of the guy on the ground ceased moving. His time was up. Indifference among those gathered was still the order of the day and I doubted any of them was aware of his change of status.

We could hear the police sirens approaching. The crowds began to slowly disperse.

As I walked home that evening, the police sirens fading in the background, I reflected on the attempted robbery and the layout of the crime scene. Was it "poetic justice" that somehow, one robber, Scorcher, died in Kingston 13, while the other, the well-dressed guy, died in Kingston 10? How Chisholm Avenue, literally and figuratively, claimed the life of another man trying to cross the divide.

I was still intrigued by the young man shot and killed by Humphrey. There were a lot of unanswered questions about him swirling in my mind: Where is he from? Why is he robbing a store with Scorcha? I thought about his mother. Does she know where her son is now? Then I thought of my own mother. She always seemed to have the answers when I needed them. This time, though, I wouldn't bother her with any of my questions about the young man. I already knew what her answer would be:

"Show me your company and I will tell you who you are."

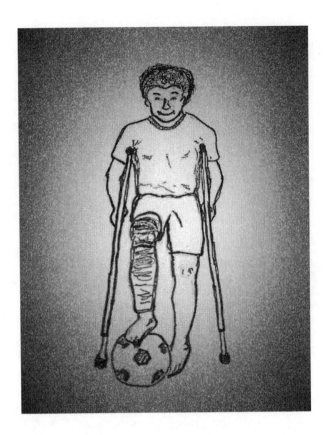

PLAY ON PLAYER!

"Young bird nuh know storm"

When I was 16 years old, I got hit by a car. It was a taxicab trying to overtake another car on a busy street. I was on the opposite side of the street waiting to cross, when out of nowhere, the taxicab appeared. That is all I remember.

My older sister, Karen, was at home sitting on the front verandah while my mother watered the flowers in the front yard and vividly remembers the events that transpired when they got the news.

"Mama was in the front yard," she recalled, "and a guy rode up on a bicycle and stopped at the gate. He had a blood-soaked shirt in his hand."

"Miss Asher!" he shouted. "See yu son shirt yah, car lick him down. " he said, as he threw the shirt over the gate to land at my mother's feet. "If him nuh dead yet, him soon dead," he stated as a matter of fact. Shaking his head in sorrow, he rode off down the road.

Mama was a country girl, brought up to speak the "Queen's English" and practice proper social decorum. She was not prone to reflexive bouts of emotional expression. This time was no different. Mama calmly picked up the bloody shirt and said she was going to get dressed. Vintage mama: no rush, no hurry. Cool and purposeful.

"Get dressed!?" A startled Karen enquired. "We need to get going now!"

"Well," mama replied, "he didn't say he was dead. So, there is still hope. I won't be long."

Karen and mama came to the hospital to find a barely conscious me, just coming out of surgery. Large lacerations on my forehead and left arm were sutured and dressed. I had a fractured femur, involving the knee joint, which was treated with immobilization via a plaster body cast that wrapped around my abdomen/torso, over my left hip, around the left leg, extending down to my toes. My right leg was not included in the cast, so there was room enough for me to perform my bodily functions. I looked like I was being mummified, and before finishing the job, the embalmer took off, leaving behind, literally, a half-assed job.

That was my life for 10 weeks. Immobilized, half of my butt exposed, confined to a bed and dependent on others for just about everything.

I should add that this was during the warm summer months, so it was hot and humid. With no air-conditioner in our home, my left leg (with the cast) was sweaty, always itching, and I was not able to scratch it. I was miserable. It felt like the biblical definition of "eternal damnation."

After the second week, the novelty of my accident wore off and my friends stopped visiting. All that remained were my three confidants: me, myself, and I. They were boring and I felt alone. This was uncharted territory for someone who was always on the move. Mama used to say that my skin would catch on fire if I stood still for too long. Well, here I was skin on fire - I had to adapt.

I now had a lot of time for introspection. This, I think in hindsight, was the best thing that came from the accident. In my solitude, I was able to hop off life's merry-go-round, look at my life and plot my future. The fragility of life became clear.

Fortunately, youth was on my side and me, myself and I adapted. I used my sister's hand mirror to look out the window and was able to see life passing by on the streets. It became my contact with the world outside. I used a pair of scissors, twisted like a drill, to bore holes, at strategic locations, into the cast. They allowed the use of a refashioned and repurposed wire clothes hanger to scratch my itchy left leg. I even learned to ease myself off the bed, put my plaster wrapped left leg on my brother's skateboard and drag myself around to the living room to watch tv.

Eternal damnation. No problem for this youth.

The ten weeks eventually came to an end. When they liberated me from that plaster cast, the first thing I noticed was that my left leg was about one-third smaller than the right. The muscles had shrunk due to dis-use atrophy. I was also unable to bend my left knee because the muscles were too weak.

My doctor prescribed a three-months course of physical therapy to strengthen the leg muscles. He also gave me a set of crutches and cautioned me not to do any walking until the physical therapy was completed, and my muscles strengthened. He also emphasized that my left knee joint would never be the same as it was before, so I should take my time with it. I clearly remembered hearing him tell mama that I would never be able to play football again. This was the worst news I could hear. No football!

The reality of our family meant that after the first few sessions of physical therapy, I was unable to make it back to the hospital for any subsequent therapy. The physical therapy seemed like a waste of time anyway. It was mostly exercises, which I could do at home, and the bus fare to go back and forth was prohibitive.

Moving around using crutches on the stony, bumpy sidewalks in my neighborhood, was uncomfortable. Within a week, I had abandoned them. I was mostly hopping around. Contrary to my doctor's orders, I was prematurely using my left knee. A sixteen-year-old youth will always push the boundaries to do what they want, and I wanted to play football. So, it was not long before I was hopping into a football game.

Eventually my hopping around matured to normal walking, and then on to running. After two months, I felt as good as new. No prescribed physical therapy. No giving the knee time to recover. All it took was the naivety of youth and my desire to play football. My doctor's advice was a distant memory and if there was no immediate pain, I would play.

There is an old Jamaican saying that goes: *"young birds nuh know storm."* Young birds have never experienced the brutal winds and downpour of a storm. It means that young people are daring, carefree, and have no fear of the dangers lurking behind their actions.

Today, over forty years later, the "young bird" who ignored his doctor's advice, continues to play football with that same knee, cranking away on the football field.

Interestingly, the current standard of care for joint injuries is early mobilization. Apparently, the sooner you get the joint moving, the better the outcome.

Thankfully, my youthful ignorance put me years ahead of my doctor on that subject. I was able to pursue my football dream and continue to live a very active life.

COLGATE TO EMIGRATE

"Suck salt outta wooden spoon"

1976 was a tough year for Jamaica, and me, personally. It was a year marred by one of the most violent political elections in the history of my beloved island. While the political drama unfolded, I was, unfortunately, confined to my bed for most of this time.

The contest between the ruling Peoples National Party (PNP) and the opposition Jamaica Labour Party (JLP) was violently displayed, for all to see, in the neighboring communities of Rema (JLP) and Concrete Jungle (PNP). There were vivid scenes of political gunmen in shoot outs with their rivals, as outgunned policemen watched from the sidelines. Stories of political gangsters and innocent civilians being murdered, families being chased out of their communities, houses being firebombed, were told daily by my high school classmates. These stories were verified by the newspaper headlines and the television news.

Word on the streets was that the atrocities were efforts to politically cleanse neighborhoods and to make it easier for Members of Parliament to retain their ministerial seats. Anyone suspected of voting for their rivals was either killed or forcibly exiled from their constituencies.

On the bigger world stage, the specter of the Cold War loomed in sunny Jamaica. The capitalist JLP was rumored to be supported by the United States and the socialist PNP by the Soviet Union, via its proxy, Cuba. The United States, it was further alleged, was determined to prevent the Soviet Union from getting another foothold in the Caribbean, via Jamaica. The USA Central Intelligence Agency was reportedly involved, and a massive campaign was deployed to undermine and destabilize the ruling, democratic socialist PNP government. Men from the volatile, Jamaican communities, on both sides of the political divide, were being armed and paid to politically cleanse and defend their communities. I had friends who were poor and unemployed, and suddenly, they were riding brand new Honda S90 motorbikes and touring with some very unsavory human elements. People who lived in these neighborhoods knew what was going on and some even wore it as a badge of honor.

Concrete Jungle (officially known as Arnett Gardens) and Rema (officially named Wilton Gardens) are stronghold communities for the PNP and JLP, respectively.

Jamaica's capital, Kingston, was besieged in terror and a State of Emergency would later be declared. The wealthy educated and skilled Jamaicans who could find work overseas were emigrating in unprecedented numbers. In fact, it seemed that anybody who could get a visa, to anywhere, was leaving Jamaica.

While this was unfolding, I was bedridden for ten weeks with a fractured femur. I came a distant second in a boxing match between me and a taxicab, on a busy street. Ten (expletive deleted) weeks on my back! I could not walk nor leave the bed. Yes, all bodily functions were performed in the bed. Indeed, a very humbling ordeal.

What this experience forced me to do, however, was to slow down, reevaluate my life and chart a course for the future. I also learned gratitude. Especially to the family members who paid me the time of day. I had a lot of time to think. My only contact with the outside world was with the people who visited, the radio, the newspapers, and a mirror I used to look, from my bed, out the front window. For a person who was always on the move, always active, and fiercely independent, the days were long, and time crept in super slow motion.

The only good news in all this came from my sister, Jennifer, who was working at the Jamaican Embassy in Washington, DC. When she heard about the accident, she invited me to visit her in the USA once I got better. It was something I had dreamt about for as long as I could remember. Every kid in Jamaica dreams about going to "'America." I saw it as an opportunity to get a first-rate education, and a first-class ticket to freedom. It would be two years later that I took Jennifer up on that offer.

Despite our proximity, visiting the USA from Jamaica is not easy if you are a Jamaican citizen. A visitors' visa is required, and getting one is not an easy task. Due to the political, economic, and social conditions in the country at the time, the USA embassy assumed that if they grant you a visa, you will not return to Jamaica. They were (and still are) very selective in who they grant visitors' visas to. You have to bring proof of "ties to the island," such as documented proof of employment; a letter from your school headmaster verifying enrollment in school (if you are a student;) land title in your name, etc. Anything to prove that you are not going to abscond once you arrive in the USA. You also need a letter of invitation from the person hosting you in the USA, and a round-trip airline ticket, to and from the USA.

Armed with your documents, you arrive at the US embassy no later than 6am. Any later you would find about three hundred people already in line, waiting. People would get up early just to hold spaces in line, and then sell their space to prospective applicants! It was first come, first served. The USA embassy is located just outside of Kingston, and people must come there, from all over the island, to apply for USA visas.

Mama took me to the embassy that morning. There were about thirty people ahead of us in line. The line was saturated with emotions.

Some people were rehearsing their presentations and preparing answers for anticipated questions. There was tension everywhere. A "visa," was for some, the last bastion of hope for personal security, for a better life, or a chance to see family and friends. For me, it opened a world of possibilities to further my education.

We made it before the consul around 2pm. I presented my passport, letter from my high school headmaster, and invitation letter from my sister, typed on official Embassy of Jamaica stationery. After a few questions.... Bam! Visa stamped in my passport. I was good to go. Baby!

As soon as we got home, I called Jennifer and gave her the good news.

I arrived in Baltimore, Maryland, in April of 1978. It was nothing like the New York that I saw on television, and as I thought all of America would be. No skyscrapers, Brooklyn Bridge, no New York taxis. I spent most of my two weeks there with my other sister, Jackie. She was closer to my age, and more importantly, her boyfriend played soccer.

Jackie's boyfriend was Richard "Bunny" Davy, a member of the Jamaican national soccer team. A legend in Jamaican soccer folklore. He was in the USA, having been awarded a soccer scholarship by Howard University (HU). During his time at HU, the soccer team would win a National Collegiate Athletic Association Division 1 Championship. To this day, that is the only NCAA division one title won in any sport, by any historically black university.

Bunny, by all accounts, was an instrumental member of that title winning team. I listened intently to his stories about his exploits on the soccer field, and he took me to play with his club team in the afternoons. I decided then that I too, was going to get a soccer scholarship from a USA university.

Life in the USA seemed surreal to me: people wore the latest fashion, the girls were all beautiful and well dressed, and the place was mostly clean. There were new, fancy cars on the roads, and you could find anything you wanted to buy in the stores. I could easily see myself living there. Oh yes, I could get into a university there with the subjects I passed in high school. Additionally, Bunny assured me, I would not have a problem getting a soccer scholarship to any of the local universities.

I went back to Jamaica to finish my last year of high school. I was confident I would return to the USA on a soccer scholarship.

The problem was, I did not have the illustrious resume of Richard "Bunny" Davy. With only one unceremonious year of high school soccer under my belt, no USA university was knocking on my door. Each time I called to ask Bunny about scholarships, the answer was no. Jackie would later confess that Bunny has a tendency for making unrealistic promises.

In 1980, another election was on the horizon and with that came the customary escalation of political violence. This time, though, it was on a higher level. Aside from the customary political gang killings, a PNP councilor was murdered while campaigning.

The incumbent Prime Minister of Jamaica, and Minister of National Security, later came under heavy gunfire during a campaign rally.

A fire destroyed a nursing home not too far from my school, killing almost one hundred-fifty elderly wards. We could smell charred flesh when we walked by the day after. Rumor had it that the fire was part of the CIA's plot to destabilize and unseat the ruling PNP.

For the previous four years, it seemed the USA had been tightening the screws on Jamaica. It appeared there was a virtual economic blockade by the USA, resulting in shortages of almost every essential item in the supermarket: Bread, flour, toilet paper, toothpaste, cigarettes, you name it, you could barely find it in Jamaica.

Between the political violence and the economic blockade, terror and desperation were the default settings for Kingston.

When I graduated from Wolmer's Boys School in 1980, I had passed four "O" level and one "A" level subjects. This was not good enough to get into any of Jamaica's two universities. In my mind, I only had one option for tertiary education - that soccer scholarship in the USA. Given the escalation in crime and violence in Jamaica, I was more determined then to continue my education overseas.

My visa from my previous trip to the USA was a one entry visitor's visa. No problem, though. It was customary that once you had received a USA visa, visited the country, and returned to the island, the US embassy would automatically renew your visa. My next step, therefore, was to return to the embassy and repeat the visa application process. This time around, my younger brother, Keith, was invited as well. This meant we both would travel to the embassy together.

My sister, Karen, who received a full scholarship to medical school in Cuba (courtesy of the close relations between Cuba and Jamaica) was home for the summer holidays. We spoke about my plans after high school and she encouraged me to head to the USA, if I could, to pursue higher education. She outlined the difficulties she experienced in Cuba and encouraged me to look at USA universities.

Karen always brought home some of her "Cuban rations" to share with the family. She usually carried toothpaste, aluminum pots, sugar, deodorant, and other little knick-knacks. Of all these items, we used the toothpaste the most. Due to the virtual economic blockade imposed by the USA, it was difficult to find toothpaste in the supermarkets. Karen brought a tube of Russian toothpaste that had a fresh minty flavor that we grew to like.

The morning when Keith and I decided to go apply for visas was routine. We got up, took our baths, brushed our teeth, gathered our documents, and made the one-mile trek to the US embassy. The process was almost the same as last time. One exception, though. Both our applications for visas were rejected.

I remember the interview very clearly. The consul leaned over the counter as he spoke to Keith and I, almost invading our personal space. I could smell his cologne and his breath too. I was very sure he could smell my breath as well. I remembered thinking, "Good thing I brushed my teeth this morning." Devoid of any emotions, the consul denied our visa application and immediately summoned the next applicant. There was no explanation or any room for discussion or questions. "Next!"

Needless to say, the walk home was a whole lot longer than the one to the embassy. As we walked under the hot midday sun, Keith and I kept wondering where it all went wrong. I had already gotten a USA visa; its renewal was usually a given. Keith was in school, doing well. Why?

We questioned everything about our presentation at the embassy: Should mama have accompanied us? We scrutinized our documents, the clothes we wore, the soap we used to bathe, down to the toothpaste we brushed our teeth with that morning.

"The Russian toothpaste! That must have been it!" I thought out loud.

"Did you see how close that guy got to us? I'm sure he could smell the toothpaste," I said to Keith, mostly in jest and trying to make light of a disappointing day.

"I wouldn't let anybody with Russian breath into my country, either, if I was working at the USA embassy." Continued Keith, keeping the deadpan humor going.

On the outside we were laughing, but on the inside, we were blown. How would we get visas to the USA? A daunting challenge for two poor Jamaican boys. Like most Jamaicans, we weren't about to throw in the towel. We would have to figure out a way to *"suck salt outta wooden spoon.*" Translation: use your creativity/abilities to make the best of a bad situation. Essentially, to get something out of nothing.

Our next order of affairs was to call Jennifer when we got home and give her the update.

I remember she found it hard to believe that we were denied visas.

"Ok, you have to go back to the embassy and reapply. If they refuse to grant you visas again, ask them why," Jennifer instructed. She also would be sending us another letter of invitation, asking the embassy to reconsider its decision.

Two weeks later Jennifer's letter arrived. Keith and I planned our trip to the embassy. Passports, Jennifer's new invitation letter, bathe, get to embassy before 6 am. This time we agreed, none of us would use the Russian toothpaste. We brushed our teeth with Colgate toothpaste that morning.

At the embassy we got the same consul who denied us visas. Just as before, he leaned into our personal space as we exchanged greetings.

"He's smelling our breaths again, " I thought.

He looked at our passports, did not bother to read Jennifer's new letter, and without asking us any questions......Bam! Bam!

A visas stamped in each of our passports!

As soon as we joyfully jumped out of the embassy, I shouted to Keith:

"I told you it was the Russian toothpaste! "

Boy! Talk about sucking salt from a wooden spoon. After all these years, Keith and I remain convinced that the Russian toothpaste was the reason the USA embassy refused to grant us visas. It was the only thing that we changed.

To this day, I still use Colgate toothpaste.

RAIN OR SHINE

"If yuh want good, yuh nose haffi run"

I first visited the US during spring, 1979, one year before graduating from high school. My eldest sister, Jennifer, was working at the Jamaican Embassy in Washington, DC. She helped me get the visitor's visa to come to the USA. It was not an easy process for a poor Jamaican to get a US visitor's visa. The prevailing sentiment was that, once I had seen the USA and all its glory, I would join the ranks of illegal immigrants and never return to Jamaica.

My other sister, Jackie, was also living in DC with her boyfriend, Richard "Bunny " Davy.

Bunny had just finished a stellar college soccer career at Howard University, which included an NCAA championship.

During my USA visit, I wound up spending most of my time in Jackie's household talking to Bunny due to our shared passion for soccer. He would take me to his twice weekly afternoon soccer practices with his club team, Universidad. The other days we played with the local Jamaicans. Universidad was a Hispanic team that paid their players for each game, so they had organized practices and meaningful drills. With the local Jamaicans it was the wild west of soccer. We just played. We played small goals, which were most often just two large rocks, separated by five- foot sizes. Anybody who showed up got to play. That meant that we could easily be playing 30 v 30, or more. Shirts v skin – One team wore shirts; the other was shirtless. Games would be competitive, and tackles were hard. These teams included national players, college players, wannabees and never was, or ever will-bees! Losing was never an option and mistakes would subject you to cussing from your teammates. Everyone wanted the ball. It was fun!

Soccer for most Jamaicans is not just a game, but a means of social interaction and to express yourself. Your prowess on the ball defines your class status on the ball field. On the field we were all equals, separated only by our footballing skills. Thankfully, I was able to hold my own amongst the best out there.

I enquired about a soccer scholarship to Howard University and Bunny assured me that I was good enough to get one.

I left the USA comfortable that I had showcased my soccer skills well enough to land a soccer scholarship to Howard University.

I returned to Jamaica, intent on making my high school football (soccer) team and to prepare for my college soccer career.

By September 1979, my spot on the Wolmer's Boys High School (WBHS) football team was secured. WBHS is a public school that is consistently rated as one of the best high schools in Jamaica and lists several Rhode Scholars among its graduates. I received a first-rate education from WBHS and felt very comfortable that I was well prepared academically for university. Now my focus would shift to official confirmation of my scholarship to Howard University.

Despite several phone calls and quite a few letters to Bunny and Jackie, there was no official word on the subject. Remember, this was 1979. There was no such thing as cellphones and the internet (as we know it today) did not exist. International phone calls were prohibitively expensive, and letters took weeks to get to the US.

"Everything cool man. Just come. You will get a scholarship." Bunny would always reassure me when we spoke. Not knowing any better, I accepted those words as a done deal. It was now May 1980. Jackie told me to apply for a new visitor's visa, which I would upgrade to a student's visa once I got the soccer scholarship.

I arrived in the USA in July of 1980. There was no soccer scholarship waiting for me. Nothing! The coach of Howard University's soccer team, Lincoln Phillips, had no idea who I was. Bunny, bless his heart, had a knack for promising more than he could deliver.

So here I was: Far away from home, unable to work, no scholarship, no anything.

Prior to my departure to the USA, I was stripped of all my worldly possessions.

"Kevin, you won't need this in America. You can get better than this ah foreign, " my friends and relatives said, as they rummaged through my belongings. I came to the USA with the clothes on my back. Plus, my soccer boots. I was not taking any chances there.

After unceremoniously burying plan A, it was now time for plan B.

With no hope of getting a soccer scholarship for that year, I shifted my attention to the following year. I contacted all the Universities within a 20-mile radius of my new home and tried to sell myself to their soccer coaches. Two local coaches expressed an interest in recruiting me. Understandably, they wanted to see me play first. The George Mason University coach invited me to visit the campus and a friend offered to take me there.

When we arrived at the campus, the coach drove us from his office to the soccer field. The soccer fields were located quite a distance from his office.

I remember two things from that visit: The gas needle in the coach's car was comfortably resting on F - full. I had never seen that before. To give you an idea of how poor we were at the time, none of my family members even owned a car. The people we knew who owned cars bought no more than five dollars of gas at a time. I even witnessed one buying seventy-five cents worth of gas, enough for one gallon of gas. This was after the gas needle had rested, in a comatose state, on "E," for several miles.

The other thing I remembered was that the visit was sometime in late fall. The leaves were off the trees, and we could see deep into the thickets of the woods surrounding the fields, where I spotted an abandoned soccer ball. It looked like it had been there for some time, given its stage of decomposition. Of course, I claimed it. No one in our household had a soccer ball at the time. It was obviously a cheap, vinyl ball with the panels at various stages of peeling off. However, I had no other ball. This was the ball that I would use to practice and prepare for my scholarship. It was practice in the mornings, by myself and kick arounds in the evenings. I had one, whole year to prepare.

At one of the kick arounds, I met a Jamaican, Patrick, who had received a soccer scholarship at the University of Maryland, College Park. He introduced me to the soccer coach at University of Maryland, who offered me a soccer scholarship after coming to see me play. It was only a tuition scholarship, but enough to get me started.

I do not remember being especially elated at the news. After all the promises from Bunny, it was more relief than anything else.

My scholarship offer letter came in March and the soccer team would begin practices at the end of July of 1981. I prepared and eagerly awaited the start of practice and the upcoming soccer season. Then, when it finally arrived, it rained nonstop for two weeks. Torrential rain! The kind of rain that flooded the roads, washed away cars, and brought traffic and commerce to a stand-still in Jamaica. Nobody left their house under those circumstances.

"Surely," I thought to myself, "there would be no soccer practice going on at the University of Maryland."

So, like any self-respecting Jamaican, I did not show up for practice those two weeks. Oh, and I did not call to find out if practice was going on, either. There was no telephone in my household when I left Jamaica, so I was not too well versed in phone etiquette. The coach was livid when I showed up for practice two weeks late. Full practices happened during the rain-storms - indoor and outdoor. In a heated tirade, he summarily kicked me off the team.

There was nothing left to say, because my pride would not allow me to see where I went wrong. An apology was not even a consideration. Just like that, my soccer career at The University of Maryland came to an unfortunate, unceremonious end.

There was some good news still: my tuition was paid for the academic year, via the soccer scholarship. Additionally, I had already registered for classes. So, of course, I attended classes for the academic year. I also found myself a part-time job.

Still fuming from the bust up with the coach, I never made any attempts to reconnect with the team. I, however, did very well that year academically and got a sense of life in an institution of higher learning. That taste fueled my hunger, and I was determined to get my degree.

By the end of the academic year, I could no longer afford to attend school at the University of Maryland and had to drop out. I used the following year to work and earn my tuition. By the time all was said and done, I had three jobs. Yes, that is right, three (expletive deleted) jobs. Do not forget that I'm a Jamaican.

I worked full-time, as a Janitor, at the Forum Condominiums, in Rockville, Maryland. I also worked part-time as a gas station attendant and did housekeeping for a family in Washington, DC.

During this time, I continued to train and play soccer with a local Jamaican soccer team, Strikers, and Universidad, a team in the Hispanic Soccer League. I was paid forty dollars per match by Universidad (so technically, I had four jobs.) Playing with the Jamaican team was primarily for bragging rights and fun. It took some serious gymnastics to make the work and soccer commitments possible. It often required some creative scheduling and thinking.

On my nightly trash emptying runs at the Forum Condominiums, for example, I would make it an actual workout. The building had seventeen floors, with stairs at each end of the floor. I would start at the first floor, sprint up the stairs to the next floor, jog to the trash room to dump the trash down the trash chute. I would then continue jogging down the hallway to the stairs at the opposite end, and repeat the process, for sixteen floors. When we cleaned the condominium's weights/exercise room we made it ours. We put the "Closed for cleaning" sign up and had a nice fifteen-minutes strength and conditioning workout. I thought I was the fittest soccer player in town. Fortunately, I was not the only one who thought so.

Howard University had a new soccer coach who was a spectator at one of my weekend games. He was impressed enough with my performance to offer me a tuition scholarship. The coach also happened to be a former team-mate of Bunny and played on that NCAA championship team. Maybe Bunny came through after all.

My dream was resuscitated with a new scholarship jolt from Howard University. I would be there, on time, for the first day of practice.

A few months before this, Jackie and Bunny convinced me to reach out to the University of Maryland's soccer coach to try to mend fences and apologize. I swallowed my pride and apologized to the coach, and we parted without animosity. No, he did not offer another scholarship, and that was okay. My visit to his office was more about gratitude, respect, and karma. One year and three jobs worth of hard labor taught me the value of a scholarship.

As the Jamaican saying goes: "*If yu want good, yu nose haffi run.*" If you want good things to happen, you must be willing to work hard and sacrifice for it.

A BALL

"Wanti, wanti can't getti, and getti, getti no wanti"

Most people who visit Jamaica invariably go to the north coast of the island where they have all the tourist infrastructure: Montego Bay, Ocho Rios, to name a few places, where there are hotels, white sand beaches and a variety of tourist attractions.

I grew up on the south coast of the island in the capital city, Kingston. Foreign tourists are advised not to travel, by themselves, to Kingston. Kingston is a mixture of South-Central Los Angeles, East Baltimore, and Bagdad, all rolled into a congested, busy, crime-plagued metropolis. Of course, the city has its uptown enclaves for the rich and wanna-be rich to inhabit.

I grew up in a tough neighborhood in Kingston. To give you an idea of how tough: at nights, when you walk the streets, you walk with money... in case you get robbed! Yup. Those crooks are professionals. You do not want to waste their time. They will either take your money and send you on your way or beat the crap out of you and warn you to walk with money next time! The streets were unpredictable, especially at night.

Within the city, the houses are typically small, and the lots are fenced to keep intruders out and to protect what's inside. The fence could be chain-linked, barbed wires, zinc sheets, cinder blocks, thorny bushes, or any combination thereof. Our home had "combination" fencing: Three feet of cinder blocks at the base that supported another three feet of chain-linked fencing on top, along the roadside of our home. Barbed wire and thorny bushes completed the perimeter and separated us from our neighbors.

Fruit trees are ubiquitous features of Jamaican homes and ours was no different. We had mango, ackee, guinep, cherry, plum, soursop, breadfruit and lime trees all packed into our tiny yard. The trees were necessary features to supplement the meager existence of the average Jamaican, but this did not leave much play space for kids, though. So, the street was our defacto playground.

My parents did not take too kindly to any of their children hanging out on "the street corners," with the neighborhood kids. My mother referred to them as idlers and did not want us to fall under their influence.

My younger brother and I would come home from school and spend hours on our tiny verandah, looking out to the street watching life unfold. Our parents forbade us from playing on the streets with the neighborhood kids, so we would dream about how we would make it out of the neighborhood. Since we were a poor family, "dream" was the operative word there.

It was on that same verandah that I came up with the bright idea to teach myself how to play football(soccer). This was how I would earn a scholarship to a university in the United States, the land where dreams come true.

I was 12 years old at the time when I conceptualized this plot for my future. Nobody in my family was remotely interested in football. I had two older brothers, one younger, four sisters, a mother and father, all of whom showed little interest in sports. I knew, from the onset, that this "dream" would be all on my shoulders.

There were some logistic issues that would have to be addressed first, though. The most important being, I needed a ball, and we could not afford one. My mother would not entertain the idea of me playing football with those "idlers" on the streets, let alone burst her meager budget to buy a ball. My father was always on the road, and he used his money to pay homage to alcohol. Up to then, we played on a side street with a makeshift ball: A pint-sized milk box, stuffed with paper. Our yards were too small to accommodate even a small-sided football game. As you might expect, none of my friends owned a real ball, either.

My aspirations for getting a football could be summarized as, "no job, no money, but no problem." I was determined to get a ball.

It took two school terms of going without lunch, walking to and from school, and saving my bus fares and lunch money. I was there:

Finally, at the end of the spring term, I had saved enough money to buy a real ball. The very next weekend, I gathered up my savings, $18.28 total, rounded up my posse, and headed uptown to buy my football.

There's strength in numbers, and in my neighborhood, when we carried valuables, there had to be more than one of us. That day, it was me, my younger brother, Keith and our friend, Michael.

Michael was one of those latchkey kids, who was always getting into trouble. My mother forbade us from going anywhere with him, because she did not want us to get caught up in the dragnet of his troubles. To me and my brother, though, his "devil-care-less" attitude was worthy of admiration. As such, he met up with us on the outskirts of our neighborhood, on our way to the sports store. His street smarts usually came in handy.

When we got to the Sports Store, we raced to the football section. The first ball I picked up had a price tag of $100. I picked up ball, after ball and the cheapest football there was $60. My enthusiasm was fading fast. Then, Michael shouted:

"What about these? "

He was rummaging through one of those large bins packed with an assortment of colorful, plastic, bouncy balls. The price tags were stuck on them. Here again, disappointment. All the football sized balls in the bin had a sticker price north of $20. Then, I found one without a sticker.

"Could this be it?" I wondered as I nervously approached the salesclerk.

"Excuse me miss; can you please tell me the price of this ball?"

"Don't you see the price sticker on the ball?" She replied dismissively. "What, yu can't read?"

Before I could gather the courage to reply, Michael gently jabbed me in the ribs and pulled me back to the bin. He discreetly peeled the sticker from a much smaller ball and pasted it to the ball I was holding. He then took the ball and my money to the cash register. I was too scared to make the purchase. My heart was beating faster than Secretariat's, right after running the Kentucky Derby. Michael calmly completed the transaction. Twelve dollars! That meant there was enough money left over to buy beef patties for all, for the long walk home.

We did not get exactly what we came for, but now I had my very own ball. Something that rolled, instead of the milk boxes that could only skid across the pavement.

We got back home about 2 pm when the sun was in its element. Too hot for street football. I placed the ball, my pride and joy, on my bed and we went to go hang out at a friend's house until the sun went down.

Sundown finally arrived and my friends and I hastily headed to my house. I was about to introduce them to my new ball.

Keith got to the verandah first and when he looked at the floor, his jaw dropped. He bent down and picked up a deflated, flaccid version of the ball I bought. We were all devastated. I later found out that my older brother, Mickey, took the ball to play with his friends. One of them kicked the ball into the bushes along the perimeter of our yard, where my ball was punctured by a thorn. I was at a loss for words. It felt like a punch to the gut from Mike Tyson (before he went to jail.) My vocal cords were paralyzed, and I could not say a word.

"Hey, we can still play with this!" One of my friends shouted.

The ball was deflated, but it was not flat. It still rolled. My dream still had a beating pulse.

"This is a hell of a lot better than the milk boxes we've been using," another added.

That evening was the beginning of a long journey for me and that ball, which would lead me to a soccer scholarship at Howard University. I still have fond memories of that ball and playing in the streets with my friends.

When my son, Daniel, was born, I wanted him to learn soccer the way I did via street style football. As soon as he could walk, he would tag along with me to the "kick arounds" with my Jamaican friends. I would also give him formal football lessons, as well.

We butted heads all the time. At twelve years old, he was convinced that he knew more about soccer than me. One incident stood out:

It was the usual soccer training in our back yard. He was about twelve years old, and we had a couple of decent soccer balls to choose from. It was a simple drill, but Daniel kept getting it wrong, over, and over. The more he messed up, the more frustrated he became. I was also losing my patience, and the scenario was becoming quite volatile. Finally, when he was at his wits end, he took the ball he was working with, hoisted into the air, and punted it deep into the bushes on the periphery of our home. Lost forever.

I immediately registered my outrage. I started yelling at the top of my voice, asking why he did that. My level of outrage seemed to surprise my son.

"Daddy, " he said, after calming down. "I don't see why you are so upset. After all, it's only a ball."

I had to restrain myself. "Only a ball!" I thought to myself, my face was red, neck veins were bulging. "Does this kid not realize that the only reason I am where I am today, is because of "a ball." Should I tell him how many weeks I went without lunch to buy a cheap, plastic version of the ball he just wasted? Maybe I should just call it a day," I pondered. Which, to maintain the peace, was exactly what I did. With ignorance this blissful, it was definitely folly to be wise, I concluded.

An old Jamaican proverb was echoing in my head, the whole time:

"*Wanti, wanti can't get it, and getti, getti, no want it.*" Those who want it, can't get it, and those who've got it, don't want it. In other words, when something comes easily, you have no appreciation for it, unlike someone who wants it, cannot afford it, and must work hard for it.

Thankfully, my son grew to appreciate the value of a ball. It paid for his undergraduate university education via a soccer scholarship. Indeed, he too, has made friends here and abroad, because of a ball.

My son now understands that to many, a ball is not "just a ball." It also represents dreams and hope. For those of us who have played "the beautiful game" of soccer, a ball also awakens memories of laughter and joy.

THE LAST THREE

"Wise monkey know what tree to climb"

My mother came from a small town in rural Jamaica. A place where one paved road ran through the entire town. Except for Saturdays, you did not see much traffic, vehicular or pedestrian, on the road. There, the houses were small and frugal. The yards, though modest in size, were verdant, and overflowing with fruit trees. You get the impression after visiting that not much, beyond the mundane, happens there.

Though my mother grew up in this pastoral setting, she did not have a "small town" mind. She was a voracious reader of books, magazines, and newspapers. Reading liberated her mind and introduced her to the outside world, its wonders, and opportunities. My mother, however, did not have the means to capitalize on those opportunities. Books were her window to a playground that she was not invited to play on. Having seen the possibilities, mama wanted her children, especially her last three, to thrive in the world she knew from reading. With her older five children in high school, she could laser focus on us.

Through her reading, Mama was well versed in all things Queens Elizabeth and Victoria, and the splendor and luxury of King Louis XIV. She also studied Latin, the root language for many Western European languages - French, Spanish and Italian, to name a few. Mama spoke only "the Queen's English," in a country where patois was the dialect of choice amongst the rural poor. She was also an ardent practitioner of proper social graces and etiquette. Though she was never snobbish, mama was aristocracy in poor woman's clothing.

Mama moved to Kingston, Jamaica's capital, after completing high school. There she excelled at secretarial school, eventually taking a position at the Ministry of Agriculture. At the Ministry, she could hold court with the elite, as well as with the common folks.

My mother had eight children who were all born in Kingston. Her children came as gender pairs: First were the twins, Jennifer, and Jean; next were Maurice and Milton (Mickey); then came Jacqueline (Jackie) and Karen; and lastly Kevin and Keith.

As best I can remember, it was my mother who did most of the parenting in our household. Our father was on the road for work quite a bit and frequented the rum bars when he was home.

Looking back, I think that my mother did a rather good job of parenting her children. Of the eight, six attended university, with five ultimately getting their university diplomas. Pretty decent return on any parent's investment if you ask me. Also, none of her kids became social delinquents or got into trouble with the law.

So, three of her children among her first five never graduated from university, mama's ultimate goal for her children. In fact, one of them did not graduate from high school at all, dropping out after second form. Another had a child born, out of wedlock, a few years after leaving high school.

Mama had lofty goals for her children. In retrospect, the perceived "shortcomings" of her first five children must have been like blasphemy to her Anglican/Victorian ideals.

By the time we, the last three, came along, I think my mother was a more seasoned parent. Mama made it clear to us, on many occasions, that we were not going to end up like our older siblings. She became more of a disciplinarian too: we had to be home before dark and chores were a must on the weekends. Our schoolwork was heavily scrutinized; homework checked; and reading emphasized. Mama even attended our school's PTA meetings. Imagine that! A working mother, practically a single parent, with eight children, making time to attend her children's PTA meetings.

Now would also be a good time to point out that Keith, Karen, and I attended three different schools.

Bear in mind also, that mama was still mother and parent, to our five older siblings. During this time mama was seeing Jean off to university and helping Jackie complete advanced level studies in high school. She was also putting what efforts she had left into getting Mickey back into school. Quite a full plate! (Jennifer and Maurice had full time jobs, so technically were off mama's books)

Mama was steadfast in her belief that she had found the formula for our success in reading.

Reading was encouraged in our household, especially for the last three. Mama made sure that we were all members of the nearby Half Way Tree public library, a trusty warehouse of books, for people who could not afford to buy books.

By the time we became members of the Library, however, books were telling different stories than those my mother read. The scent of Jamaica's independence, a decade earlier, still lingered in the air. The Rastafarian movement and its Afrocentric, anticolonial rhetoric was gaining the attention of Jamaica's youth. The news broadcasts were consistently covering the African continent's struggle for independence. Revolution and rebellion were in the air. The reggae group, Bob Marley and the Wailers, rose to prominence during this time. Their anti-colonial, social justice music dominated Jamaica's airwaves. The luster of the British and French empires, along with their Iconic Queen Victoria and King Louis XIV, was fading. We would not be reading our mother's books or honoring her heroes.

Karen gravitated towards the Nancy Drew, female heroine types of books. Keith was into all books sci-fi and was an ardent Star Trekker. I never read any books at all. My heart and sentiments were with the Rastas and African revolutionaries. I would not allow myself to be indoctrinated with US or European ideology, by reading their propaganda (a.k.a. books). This is how I justified not reading books, to my mother. The truth was, I hated reading. I could not sit still long enough or had the patience for reading. Even if I tried. I usually became bored after the first paragraph! Sports and competition were my things. I had to be in motion.

My lack of interest in reading irritated mama. I would have a million excuses not to read, even when I sat around on the verandah doing nothing. Then, mama and I would have heated debates about what exactly constituted time wasting: (reading, for me; hanging out doing nothing, for her.)

Mama does not surrender easily, though. She pulled rank and forced me to read articles from the sports section of the newspaper. I had to do this every weekend. She knew that I loved sports. It was a chore at first, but it sucked me in slowly, as I kept up with the local football league. While reading sports articles, often articles from other sections of the newspaper would pique my interest. Before long, I was reading most of the newspaper. I never migrated to reading novels, or books, as my mom hoped, but at least I was in the queue to read our daily newspaper. My experience reading the newspapers also made the mundane task of reading textbooks from school less of a chore. I am sure I speak on behalf of Keith and Karen on that point. By the way, Karen and Keith are both, to this day, avid readers of books. Score another one for the mamster!

Mama introduced us to reading as youngsters and prioritized our education. Reading, regardless of the medium or genre, is the pathway to education. When both are emphasized at an early age, the outcome is phenomenal. Education has the power to change lives in the present, and the fortunes of future generations. Our accomplishments in academia were built on the foundation laid by our mother. These educational achievements significantly changed our lives in a positive manner.

Mama, who had only a high school diploma herself, lived to see five of her children achieve advanced university degrees.

I cannot say much about what happened with my older siblings, because I wasn't around for most of that saga. It was clear that her experience with them and the wisdom garnered was of benefit to Keith, Karen, and I.

As the old Jamaican saying goes: *"wise monkey know what tree to climb."* Wisdom and experience help you to achieve your goals. Mama, our wise monkey, led us to the trees of reading and education. Her endeavors on our behalf paid dividends and spawned three successful careers.

So much so, that we have written our own version of the Tinker Tailor* counting rhyme:

> A rich man was a poor man,
> No beggar, nor thief.
> Keith became a lawyer.
> Karen is a doctor,
> Kevin the dentist, fix Indian teeth.

Yes, horrible joke, but I am LOLing (I know, also not funny!)

- Tinker Tailor counting rhyme:

    "Richman, poor man, beggar man, thief
     Lawyer, doctor, Indian chief."
    It is commonly used for counting out, for example who is "it" in a game.

NUCLEAR FUSION

"Shine eye gal is a worry to a man"

I met Laura at Howard University, in Washington, DC. She was a freshman taking advanced level molecular microbiology, and I, a senior, was desperately trying to graduate and get out of school. Neither of us were supposed to be in that class.

As a freshman, Laura was to have taken the required/prerequisite, introductory microbiology classes first, which she had not done. I needed to fulfill my required credits in microbiology and since the class was full, I had to plead my case to the professor and beg my way in. I was the last person to get in the class and shared a lab bench with Laura. She was a beauty. I almost got whiplash when she sat down beside me. We hit it off immediately. Two foreign students who shared similar views on geopolitics and humanity. We ate lunch and hung out together and read each other's poems. Beethoven's fifth symphony played in the background when we were together. It was destiny.

Then, before I could exhale, she left. Laura returned to Cameroon, answering her father's call to come home. Her father needed her in Cameroon, to sort out some family affairs. It was an edict written in stone. In a matter of days, Laura and all her worldly possessions were heading back to Cameroon. The music was gone.

I never heard from her again, until about eight months later, I received a letter from Cameroon. Laura was living, alone on a farm, in the jungle of Cameroon. Her relationship with her father had deteriorated and she was in self-imposed exile on the farm. Oh, yes, ...and she missed me.

Well, that got my heart pumping. Over several more letters, I gathered my meagre savings and offered to buy her a ticket to return to the US.

After the expected and obligatory, "no, I can'ts," she was on her way back to the USA. My sister, Jackie, was kind enough to allow her to live with us for a while, until we eventually found an apartment of our own.

We were so compatibly incompatible; it was not funny. Our horoscopes even told us this in no uncertain manner. According to Chinese astrology, ours were the most incompatible zodiac signs. I could hear Confucius saying: "Man who take incompatible wife, bound to live miserable life!"

So, what did we do? We got married anyway. Thus began our take of a classic romantic tragedy, that I titled: "Foolio and Juliet." (You do not have to ask who Foolio in that drama was.)

As a couple, we got along very well about forty percent of our time together. The other times we were like two positively charged, strong-willed atoms trying to come together. When we brought our collective forces together, however, the results were powerful, like nuclear fission energy.

Nuclear fission is how energy is generated by nuclear power plants and nuclear weapons. It is a nuclear reaction in which a heavy atomic nucleus splits, on impact, into two or more lighter nuclei, releasing a great amount of energy. Boom!

Ours was a mushroom cloud that produced a dental degree for me, a medical and divinity degree for her, five well accomplished children and the so-called material trappings of success. At the end of the day, though, it was a lot of work making it through the challenging times.

To me, sometimes it felt like trying to achieve nuclear fusion energy (the opposite of fission.)

Nuclear fusion occurs when you expose small atoms, like hydrogen, to incredibly high temperatures and pressure, over a long period of time. These conditions create plasma, the fourth state of matter, where the fusion of two or more atomic nuclei can occur, releasing vast amounts of nuclear energy. It produces way more energy than nuclear fission, minus the harmful, radioactive by-products. No current model exists on earth, that can efficiently achieve these conditions. They put more energy into the system (via electricity to generate the temperature and pressure necessary to create plasma) than what is generated from the actual nuclear fusion.

This is how complicated my marriage felt during our hard times. I use this analogy because both marriage and nuclear fusion have baffled scientists for ages. To me, they are both "rocket science."

There is a popular Jamaican saying that often came to mind, as I struggled to make my marriage work: "*A shine eye gal is a worry to a man.*" There have been many Jamaican songs that lament the "shine eye gal" experience. According to Jamaican folklore, "Shine eye gal," or pretty girls, are accustomed to, and usually crave attention and adulation. They are "high maintenance," needy, and never satisfied. Shine eye gals usually get their way and, also, attract a band of suitors. This, understandably in any relationship, can be worrisome to their mates.

Nonetheless, having strong beliefs in the institution of marriage, we tried our best.

Roughly twenty-eight years and five children later, Laura decided she no longer wanted to be married (to me, at least) and filed for divorce. Ironically, this happened a few months after she received her divinity degree and became an ordained minister. Maybe it was "divine" intervention. Who knows?

It was not the ending that I wanted, or envisioned, but in hindsight, it was time for us to go our separate ways.

I will be the first to admit that I was not that perfect husband from the wedding manual. I am sure Laura had her many valid reasons for leaving the marriage. To friends and family, the end of the marriage seemed like something out of the blue. To be honest, it felt that way to me as well. Like any other marriage, we had our fair share of ups and downs and disagreements. I viewed the period prior to the divorce as just another phase for us to get through.

Laura, for her part, discreetly did her research, and formulated her exit strategy. When it was time to pull the plug, all her ducks were in a row. It was "shock and awe" to me, though. I knew exactly what Saddam Hussein was going through when the US was bombing Baghdad!

The divorce, to continue the nuclear analogy, was like nuclear fall-out, the radioactive dust from the mushroom clouds created by nuclear fission explosions. When that dust falls out of the sky back to earth, it spreads radiation wherever it settles. The divorce was messy, costly, and lasted years. There were child custody hearings, which included social workers sniffing around my house. They came to see if the house where my daughter, Guemana (affectionately called Gigi,) lived happily for ten years, was suitable for her to live, post-divorce. We even had to attend mandatory parenting classes (taught by someone young enough to be my child, who looked like she could use some parenting, herself.) Multiple court appearances followed that involved our children. All the intimate details of our lives were laid bare in court, for the world to see. In retrospect, the only people who benefited from our divorce were the lawyers. Laura's lawyer moved into a brand-new office in an expensive neighborhood, a few months afterwards. According to rumors, mine was shopping for a new car.

After our assets were divided, I was left with an "underwater" home (one valued far less than the mortgage owed on it,) with a high interest rate. Also, my credit score took a nose dive because no mortgage payments were being made during the divorce. My nuclear fall-out lingered way beyond the divorce and it took years to repair my credit and refinance the house. It was important for me to keep this house to maintain some semblance of continuity and stability for the children in the aftermath of a contentious divorce. Tough decision, but no regrets.

During, and after the divorce, I remembered being depressed and feeling like an absolute failure. My daily routine was literally, from bed to work and back to bed again. In my head, everything that I spent the last twenty-odd years building was dismantled. If I did not have bills to pay, it would have been bed to bed and back to bed again. There were way more bad days, for me, than good days. I did not want to face the world, or the world to see me. My ego and self-esteem were intimately woven into the fabric of my marriage, and it had rotted. I was sure Elisabeth Kubler-Ross was talking about me to my friends.

Yes, the "On Death and Dying" author was giving me her undivided attention.

As time passed, I realized that I did not have a monopoly on shame and suffering. My children, my family, and I'll guess, my ex-wife, were also grieving. It seemed ok to feel sorry for myself, but I had to get it together for the children, especially Gigi. The divorce helped me identify my true friends, acquaintances, and the band-wagonists. After a while, it became easier to accept that it takes two individuals to make a marriage work. It was at this point that I started having more good days than bad days.

It is said that time heals all wounds and mitigates fall-out damage. Today there is no bitterness towards my ex-wife, and overall, I have no regrets. We had many great times and accomplished a lot together. I am grateful for our union that produced five wonderful children.

Now that the toxic dust has settled from the divorce, I feel liberated. I had spent so many years attending to family needs and trying to make the marriage work, that my inner muse was neglected - starved of oxygen. I can inhale now. Poetry is in my books again and comedy classes are next. I am also seriously thinking of writing a book!

I have often been asked if I would ever remarry. When I ponder this question, the concept of nuclear fusion comes back to mind. Nuclear fusion is the holy grail of clean energy production. It is the process that powers the sun, producing an endless output of energy. It would be a game changer to replicate this on earth, and commercially produce an endless supply of clean energy. Goodbye Middle East, hello Fusion Energy. Nirvana!

Yet, after decades of trying and billions of research dollars invested, nuclear fusion energy has proven to be a formidable and elusive task. Thus far, it has been such an expensive, technically complicated, and frustrating process, that many think it is impossible.

I find it ironic that I could use those same adjectives to describe my marriage: complicated, frustrating, expensive, and ultimately, impossible. So, when scientists on earth figure out how to produce efficient nuclear fusion energy, that is when I will try my hand again at marriage.

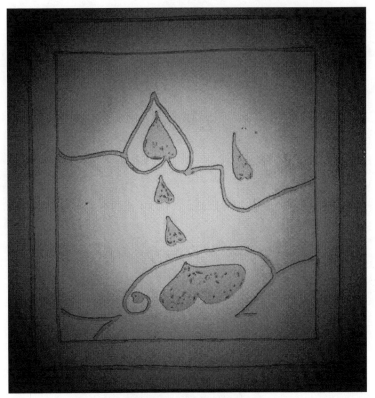

TALK IS CHEAP

"Oily tongue nuh mus tell truth"

The Chinese in Jamaica employ one of the oldest and most successful business formulas that I have ever seen: They come together in groups and put a fixed sum of money into a weekly pool. Each week, a different individual from the group takes home the money in the pool. This continues until every member of the group has had their "draw" from the pool. Every week, a different member of the group will collect a lump sum of money to use as they please. This money is often used to buy or lease a place in a commercial district. They then establish a business (retail store or restaurant, usually) on the ground floor, living quarters will be upstairs and the parents and children work in the business. Their business overhead is technically their mortgage; employees are never late, and business fraud is typically not an issue.

Even in crime infested neighborhoods, their businesses have managed to thrive.

If there is the need to employ a local person, two things are readily apparent. First and foremost, that local person cannot touch the cash register. Only family members are entrusted with that privilege. Secondly, the local person hired, is usually a female. They view local females as more dependable and less threatening workers.

Back in my youthful days, the boundaries between employers and employees were not as well defined as they are today. Invariably, you would hear rumors of flirtations and outright affairs between Mr. Chin and his female employees. (Chinese/Orientals are referred to loosely as Mr. or Ms. Chin. Jamaicans consider this respectful, since formal titles, Mr. or Ms. are used.)

When I was a teenager, I sometimes used to hang out on the street corner (against my parents' wishes) with my friends, after school. We caught up on the latest gossip, hollered at the young ladies passing by, exchanged jokes, and horsed around. There was one guy, a few years older than us, who always had a good joke to tell. We called him George Worse, or Worse for short. One of the best footballers in the world during that time was the Irishman, George Best. Our friend was so horrible at football that we named him George Worse, and the name stuck. To this day, he is affectionately known to everyone as "Worse." I do not think that his mother remembers his real name. I certainly do not.

One evening, George Worse came on the corner and told us a joke about Mr. Chin and his Jamaican employee/lover. Two reliable ingredients for a great joke in Jamaica. However, the joke bombed. Nobody laughed, except Worse. In his head, it was the funniest joke he ever told. He was still laughing as he walked away into the sunset. It was as if he knew something that we did not.

About five years later, I finally got the joke and was able to appreciate why Worse was the only one laughing. In fact, I think the joke is so funny and practical that I have told it to all my children.

The joke was about Mr. Chin, a dry goods store owner. After months of flirtations and innuendos, Mr. Chin was finally able to get Beverly, his employee, upstairs into his bed. Beverly did not disappoint. She gave Mr. Chin the sex of his life! So mesmerizing was the sex that he was screaming and hollering the whole time.

"BEVERLY! BEVERLY! EVERYTHING DOWNSTAIRS IS YOURS! EVERYTHING DOWNSTAIRS IS YOURS.

THATS RIGHT, EVERYTHING DOWNSTAIRS IS YOURS!" Mr. Chin shouted.

Mr. Chin was repeating those lines like a broken record, raising the volume as the seconds raced by. By the time he climaxed, Mr. Chin was so exhausted that he quickly fell asleep.

The next morning Mr. Chin woke up to find Beverly downstairs, rearranging the entire store.

"Beverly!" He shouted angrily; "What you doing!?"

"But, Mr. Chin, Last night you said that everything downstairs was mine," a bemused Beverly replied.

"That was f*ck talk!" Mr. Chin hissed his teeth and responded in disbelief. "That was f*ck talk!"

"Put back mi merchandise," he continued.

The humor and moral of that story came to me after I left home and started college. I was on my own and forced to accept people for who they are and see the world as it is. I quickly found out that there are no guarantees when it comes to promises. It does not matter who they are or where they're from. In the euphoria of the moment, there are people who will promise you any and everything. They will be so convincing that, to the uninitiated, it becomes gospel. However, once the euphoria fades and reality sets in, they are often unwilling to make good on said promises. Often, you never hear from them again.

Part of maturity and growth as an individual, is the ability to distinguish a genuine promise, with commitment, from "f*ck talk." I am grateful to George Worse for helping me to recognize the difference. My mother taught me countless old Jamaican proverbs. One such proverb being: *"Oily tongue nuh mus tell truth."* An oily tongue doesn't always speak the truth. Basically, to beware of smooth talkers. I have also grown to appreciate the value in these Jamaican sayings.

The Mr. Chin story drove the point home. As soon as my kids reach eighteen years of age, I tell them this story. It has become a rite of passage. They must know that if talk is cheap, then f*ck talk is even Worse.... (Corny, but I could not resist.)

DREAM KETCHER

"Ol' fire stick easy fi ketch"

A "dream-catcher" is a Native American spiritual ornament hung over a bed that, according to custom, is supposed to protect you from bad dreams, enable good dreams to materialize, and filter out negative energy. It basically is a circle with cobweb designs across its center and feathers hanging from it. My daughter, Chiny, had one hanging in her room that her mother, Laura, placed there when she was an infant. It was there for several years until it became a tattered, worn eyesore. Since I didn't have much faith in the powers of those type of things, I snatched the unsightly ornament and hid it in a closet. Nobody knew that I was the one who took it. "What does a nine-year-old girl have to dream about anyway?" I rhetorically asked myself. Many years later, I would get my answer.

Against my advice, Laura, signed Chiny up to play on a recreational soccer team. Recreational soccer, from my perspective, was a wasteland of players signed up by their parents, to play a game they are not keen on playing. Half the kids involved are only there because their parents signed them up and made them play. I also thought that soccer was a dead-end sport for girls and that Chiny would be better off running track. We already had another daughter, Mponya, doing track so it would be easy for her to get off the mark there, and transportation wouldn't be an issue. With four very active kids, we needed to be efficient with our time and resources. (Her other older siblings, Imani was doing Poms, and Daniel, travel soccer.)

Travel soccer for her older brother, Daniel, was already consuming a lot of my spare time. His practices were about 20 miles from home and took us through a rush-hour quagmire three times a week. The idea of taking another child to practice and games was not something I was willing to entertain. Laura insisted, however, and Chiny would get her first taste of competitive soccer. Laura signed her up, so she became the driver and coach for Chiny's initial foray into soccer. That was our compromise.

I was so consumed with Daniel's games and practices that I never had the time, (or perhaps the will,) to attend Chiny's games. As the season came to an end, however, I had to at least make it to her last game. I would not be able to live in our house if I missed her entire first season of soccer.

I remember leaving right after Daniel's game was over and heading straight to Chiny's game. We arrived midway into the first half. When I got to the field, her team was being killed by the opposing team, 3-0. It was mostly a one-sided game, but two of the girls on the team were outstanding though: the coach's daughter, and Chiny. You could see potential in these two. The coach had this to say about her after the game:

"She covers a lot of ground and she doesn't give away the ball to the other team."

At the recreational soccer level, where most kids chase the ball like a pack of wolves after meat, and kick it in no particular direction, this was a huge compliment.

I also saw Chiny trying to incorporate some of the moves I had been teaching Daniel, into her play. Clearly, she had been taking notes while I was coaching Daniel.

The next season, Chiny's soccer coach moved up to coach a more advanced travel soccer team and brought his daughter and Chiny to the new team. We bought her a brand-new pair of soccer cleats for the new season, but she hardly wore them. She chose instead to wear a pair of hand-me-downs from Daniel: they were Adidas Predators, the type of cleats worn by the iconic player, David Beckham. I never knew what a pair of Predators looked like with shoe polish until Chiny inherited hers. She adored those cleats.

I could no longer ignore Chiny's soccer potential and the hunger and passion she displayed for the game. It was not long before I took her under my wings, including her in my coaching sessions with Daniel. You could tell that Chiny loved soccer by the enthusiasm that she brought to practice. She came to our sessions prepared; there were no arguments nor complaints, just a willingness to learn and improve. She was a quick study and a refreshing change from her brother. I would sometimes spend half our coaching sessions arguing with Daniel. I even fired him on a few occasions, swearing each time, never to waste my time coaching him again. Of course I would resume coaching Daniel – somebody had to have sense for him until he developed his own sense! Chiny, on the other hand, was a joy to coach.

After her second season of travel soccer ended, Laura signed Chiny up for track and field during the summer break to keep her active. Here again, she excelled. So much so that we kept her in track full-time.

Her first two years into track saw her develop into an outstanding middle to long distance runner, winning medals at the state, regional and national levels. She was blooming into such a good runner that track coaches were already scouting her.

Training and traveling to track meets consumed just about all of Chiny's spare time, but she still played for a local soccer team that was willing to accommodate her track schedule. You got the feeling, however, that the pecking order should be reversed: soccer first, track second. One doesn't argue with success though, and successful she was on the track. With the accolades from track piling up, soccer remained in the background, strumming louder and louder on her second fiddle.

Deep inside, Chiny's passion was for soccer. It was like track was her husband from a marriage her parents arranged, and soccer was the lover that she really cherished. Whenever she found time, she would solicit my help for soccer workouts. These sessions were like an illicit lover's rendezvous. When it was my time to pick her up, we would often do soccer work outs after track practice in the evenings. Often till darkness made it impossible for us to continue. We would do these workouts secretly. Her mom and/or the track coaches could not know about these workouts, because they thought I would be physically "overloading" Chiny and it would negatively affect her performance on the track.

At age 16 years old, she was allowed to choose her primary sport and I had no doubt what her choice would be. Chiny's love of soccer was an open secret, and when she chose to divorce herself from track completely and pursue soccer full time, there were no surprised faces. Jamaicans have an old saying that comes to mind when I think of this period of Chiny's soccer career: *"Ol' fire-stick easy fi ketch."* (old fire stick easy to catch) It simply means that it is easy to start a fire with wood that was previously in a fire (ol' fire stick.) The phrase is used to explain why it is so easy to rekindle an old romance. Her first love was soccer and it was not hard for her to restart that love affair. Chiny's ultimate goal was to play soccer at the highest level possible at the time: a top ranked US college, where the best women's soccer in the world was being played. This was the dream that she prayed her dream-catcher would filter when it hung over her bed many years earlier.

When she returned full time to travel soccer, her ol' fire stick got spontaneous ignition. In no time she polished her rusty skills, and quickly became a consistent starter on her new team, Freestate United. Her years in track and field, however, prevented the exposure necessary to get recruited by major colleges, let alone get offered a soccer scholarship.

By her senior year, no major college soccer program had expressed an interest in her, and the window of opportunity was closing. Meanwhile, several of her team mates had already been offered and accepted college soccer scholarships to those institutions. It was a very frustrating time for Chiny to watch her teammates add "committed" to their player profiles and she was not even getting any attention. No disrespect to her teammates, but when you are showing so much love for the sport, and soccer was not reciprocating, it gets to your head.

To us, something just did not seem right. Here we had a good, technically proficient player, and a great athlete, yet no scholarship offer. We had done the usual stuff to attract the attention of college coaches: emails, phone calls, send her bio and DVDs, to no avail. The coaches all said that they had to see her in action, but never came to watch her play. With time running out, anxiety was consuming Chiny. She was losing sleep over the matter and her hair was falling out in clumps. It even began to negatively affect her relationship with her coach…me!

Her training sessions with Freestate were becoming exercises in futility and her lack of motivation and petulance was spilling over into the sessions she had with me. I cannot tell you how many times I was tempted to tell her to stop acting like a female dog (spelled with a capital B!) It's tough sometimes to be a parent and a coach to your own children.

I had to constantly remind Chiny to stop thinking of herself as a victim of the college recruiting system and to see the opportunity that her "uncommitted" status presented. Since many of the top players had multiple scholarship offers from multiple colleges, then there would be programs that would not be able to sign some of their recruits. These programs would then be looking at the pool of uncommitted players to fill out their rosters. I reassured her that coaches were still recruiting to prepare for the aforementioned scenario. It was up to her then, to remain focused and prepare for the next showcase tournament.

Next up on the calendar was the Girls College Showcase, in Raleigh, North Carolina. It is held annually during December and is arguably the last tournament before coaches send out their scholarship offer letters to recruits. Since this was Chiny's senior year in high-school, that tournament was perhaps her last shot at a soccer scholarship. I did not want to put too much pressure on her, but this was a very important tournament for her. Needless to say, we wanted to be prepared for this tournament, and formulated a plan of action.

Our plan was to improve Chiny's physical endurance and sharpen her technical skills. When she got to that tournament, she should be able to hold onto the game ball like it was her own and beat her defenders at will. The coaches would have no choice but to take notice of her soccer skills. In sports, the eyes always follow the ball.

Not as easy as it sounds, though. It required her to change her approach to the game away from a "pass first," to "dribble first," mentality, and to develop the more refined motor skills needed for dribbling. All this in four weeks. It would likely mean that she would have to ignore her coaches and the cries from the sidelines for her to pass the ball. Not easy for a 17-year-old used to obeying her elders, but she was up for the challenge.

By early November, everything was going as planned. Chiny was in good physical condition; her stamina and endurance were significantly improved and her dribbling skills were coming along as well. The road to Raleigh seemed bright and sunny.

Then came the change back from daylight saving time to eastern standard time. The time change did not leave me with enough daylight after work to practice with Chiny. By the time I got home from work it was too dark to have any meaningful practices. To make matters worse, during that month, rain showers, especially on the weekends, would visit our neighborhood, and make a swamp of our practice field.

Chiny began to get demoralized. From her time in track, she understood how weeks of inaction would negatively affect her performances.

"There is nowhere for us to practice or workout," she lamented. Her eyes looking like a dejected puppy searching for its mother. "I always have the worst luck," she continued. Before she could wander any further along that path of negativity, I cut her off.

"Darkness, rain or even a total eclipse of the sun, we will have to figure out a way for you to practice and stay in shape," I told her. "The coaches won't care why you couldn't practice," I continued. "They are recruiting the player they see on the day. Our job is to make sure the coaches see a scholarship worthy player in you at that tournament." I had to remind her that she is a good soccer player and to be more positive and optimistic.

While sitting by my window one afternoon watching the pouring rain create a pond in the backyard, I was desperate for answers to where we could resume our training sessions.

"Chiny," I asked. "Where can we find a place where there is light when I come home from work, that is warm, and we don't have to worry about the rain?"

"I dunno," she replied. "Inside the house, maybe." She tilted her head to the side and shrugged her shoulders as part of her sarcastic answer.

Believe it or not, that was the answer. Inside the (expletive deleted) house!

"Why did I not think of this before?" I asked a bemused Chiny, who seemed embarrassed that I was even entertaining her silly suggestion.

With nothing better to do that weekend, I moved some furniture around to clear a running path and maximize our basement space. While stuffing furniture in the closet, I noticed that the old, battle-scarred dream-catcher was still there, in the same place I hid it years ago.

"Time to dust it off and hang it up again," I thought.

I am not an overtly superstitious person, but this was one of those WTF/nothing to lose moments. So the dream-catcher was brought out from exile and hung from the basement ceiling.

Our in-house training routine consisted of the following: stretching, exercising, and running up and down two flights of stairs. Next it was to the basement for wall to wall running, practice passing, ball control, and dribbling. We did this, two hours per day, for three weeks prior to the tournament. The limited space in the basement was challenging at first, but after a while Chiny adapted and grew quite adept at playing in tight spaces. With the basement being the only available playing field, her soccer starved brother, Daniel, would join us on occasions so we could tag team Chiny. Three weeks later, she was perhaps the fittest player on her team.

Our Raleigh tournament plan worked to perfection. The coaches of Purdue University were walking by one of Chiny's game, saw her running rings around her opponents and offered her a scholarship at the tournament.

In their conversation afterwards, she asked one of the coaches why they were so eager to offer her a scholarship on the spot in Raleigh. He said that he and his coaches were on their way to scout another player and were walking past her game. Chiny was with the ball, and two opposing players were forcing her into the corner, like hyenas closing in for a kill. That set-up gets every coaches attention, so they paused to watch the scenario unfold.

How she deftly managed to get out of that tight spot, the ball still at her feet, defenders in the background, is what captured his interest. "You don't usually see that type of skill from girls, at least not in the US," he stated.

While they were convinced that Chiny had already "committed" to a university, they still wanted to find out more about the unusual player they just saw. In reading her player profile booklet (provided by the Freestate United team manager,) they were surprised that she was listed as "uncommitted." After further enquiries, watching her other games, and speaking with Chiny, the coaches knew that they had to act swiftly. Hence the scholarship offer at the tournament.

Looking back at the events leading up to the Raleigh tournament, it almost seems as if there was a Devine plan in place (maybe that dream-catcher was working its magic as well.)

I was among the naysayers when Chiny initially expressed her interest in soccer. Thankfully, her mother persisted and got her involved with youth soccer, stoking her passion for the game. When she returned to travel soccer, after the hiatus in track, her ol' firestick was easy fi ketch, and she easily reintegrated back into the game.

Her time on the track circuit was not for naught as it taught Chiny the value of practice and preparation. There she would often hear the phrase, *"If you fail to prepare, then prepare to fail."* This was the work ethic she brought back to soccer that made her excel.

Surely it was not by coincidence that the outdoor conditions leading up to the tournament were dismal. Those conditions forced us to train regularly in our small, cramped basement. Chiny was comfortable getting out of that tight corner during that game in Raleigh because she had practiced that scenario many times before with Daniel and I in our basement.

When preparation meets opportunity, good things usually happen. In our case, it meant that Chiny would realize her dream of playing for a major collegiate soccer program. Purdue University is one of the top academic universities in the USA (ranked #43 by US News, 2023) and competes in the "Big 10," a NCAA division 1 conference. Big 10 universities are always at the forefront of college sports in the USA and have some of the best athletic facilities in the world (that's right, the world.) The conference is also among the best for women's college soccer.

I often reflect on this phase of Chiny's life journey because it was a humbling experience for me. Had it not been for her mother, I could have killed her soccer dream by discouraging her from participating in the game in the important formative years. This introspection has enabled me to learn and grow from that experience and I am now fully committed to supporting my children's sporting ambitions. With my help, they will rise or fall, based on their talents and initiatives. In fact, If Chiny were ever to say that she wants to play in the Women's World Cup, I would be right there by her side supporting her…darkness, rain, or total eclipse of the sun.

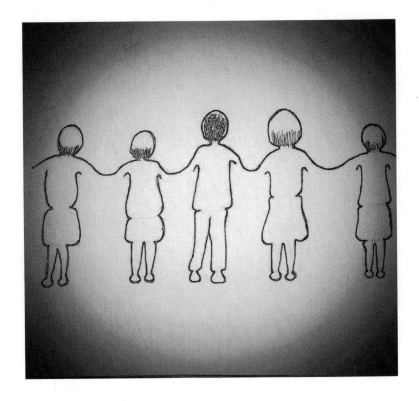

MILLENNIAL SEEDS

"Bend the tree when it young, when it old it wi bruk"

It's close to midnight and I am suddenly awakened to the wailing cries billowing out of my daughter's mouth as she tried to wiggle her way out of my arm. Her brother who was asleep on my other arm had also woken up. Like a choir member on cue, he was now screaming. We had all fallen asleep in an old Lazy-Boy recliner, a child on each of my arms, watching tv. The Nightly News was broadcasting graphic images of the war in Iraq. As I got up to turn off the TV set, I peered out the apartment window to the concrete and asphalt landscape below, where my eyes were drawn to the flashing blue lights. Outside below my window, a crowd of teenagers were shouting at the police as they lead Devon, a known drug dealer, to the back seat of a police cruiser. A shootout between rival drug dealers last night was probably the reason why the police were there.

Meanwhile, my children were still screaming, now at a higher pitch than before. As I rushed to comfort and quiet them, I tripped on something from the minefield of litter spread across the room and hit the floor. Thud!

The crying stops for a moment but resumes as soon as my children realize that I'm still alive.

Outside there was chaos. Inside there was chaos!

"Is this what I left Jamaica for?" I ask myself.

The following is my journey through the chaotic millennial years, and that of my five children who showed up for the ride.

1980 is the year that has been dubbed by experts, as the beginning of the millennial generation. Those born between the years 1980 to 2000 are members of the millennial generation. That title was bestowed because they are the generation who would become the leaders of the world in the twenty-first century, the new millennium. This era (1980 - 2000) was a time of great social and economic turmoil in the world. Due to advances in technology, it was possible to witness disruptive, local, and international events in real time, as they unfolded - the good, the bad and the ugly!

1980 saw me sitting in a two-bedroom apartment in the Washington, DC metro area, which I shared with my sister and her family. I was mostly watching TV, because I had nothing better to do. I was not enrolled in school, as I had planned, and I had no job or means of transportation. I was considered by some (including myself,) a failure and a waste of public funds. Making any progress from there would be extremely difficult, given the depressing socio-economic climate in the USA. I was ready to abandon my "American Dream," and move back to my native Jamaica. My native Jamaica, however, did not want me back. At least, not as a failure. Everyone I spoke to in Jamaica made that clear to me, in no uncertain manner.

So here I was, thrown into the ocean called the USA, where it was "sink or swim," and I didn't know how to swim.

The millennial years highlighted the failures of communism as an economic model and oversaw the transition from the government planned economies to private laissez-faire capitalism. These transitions were often precipitated by means of violent, popular insurrections.

Millennials were born to the noise of deconstruction and reconstruction. They bore witness to the dismantling of the Soviet Union (USSR,) Yugoslavia and Czechoslovakia. With the breakup of the Soviet Union, the cradle of communism, the US became the world's only superpower.

Also on display was the carnage of chemical weapons, used by Iraqi leader, Saddam Hussein, on Iranians during the Iran-Iraq war of the 1980s. The intifada uprising in the Palestinian territories of the West Bank and Gaza Strip was must-see for anyone with a television set or a computer. Buildings in the Middle East were reduced to rubble during war time and resurrected after treaties were signed between the warring factions.

Millennials would have an up to the minute view of these proceedings with the roll out of twenty-four-hour cable news channels. The development of the internet, the world wide web and hand-held video recorders also gave us front row access to the world's trouble spots, 24/7. We became emotionally invested in these worldwide dramas, as a result. We could see the suffering and feel the pain.

Acquired immune deficiency syndrome (AIDS) was formally recognized as a disease and became a worldwide phenomenon, to begin the eighties. You watched people wither into emaciation and a slow, guaranteed death. It was considered a queer/junkie disease until basketball legend, Magic Johnson, and tennis great, Arthur Ashe, contracted the disease. It got the world's attention, research funding and effective treatments thereafter.

Images of the devastating famine in Ethiopia (1983-85) led to the assembly of over forty-five of America's top recording artists to record the single, "We are the World." That record sold over twenty million copies, with the bulk of the proceeds going towards the Ethiopian famine relief efforts. Images of those starving children would not allow us to sit this one out.

The fall of Apartheid in Southern Africa was on in earnest during this time. First with the independence of Rhodesia, renamed Zimbabwe (1980), followed by Namibia (1990) and finally the fall of apartheid in South Africa. Then, after much anticipation, Nelson Mandela was freed in 1990. Mandela's release, after twenty-seven years of imprisonment, was the final nail in Apartheid's coffin and sparked worldwide celebrations.

The world watched as USA space shuttles flew to space and back to earth, on multiple occasions, underscoring America's dominance in outer space.

We also watched the speech in Berlin, at the Brandenburg gate, by USA President Ronald Reagan (1987), which led to the demolition of the Berlin Wall and ignited the peaceful re-unification of East and West Germany.

Change and transition were the order of the day during the millennial years. Cable news and the internet brought it before our eyes and closer to home. Technology brought the world closer, creating a global community with the USA as its de facto leader.

This should have been a great time to be in the USA. Yet, all was not well on the American front. The USA would not be immune to the chaotic changes affecting the rest of the world.

I bore witness to the reality of this America, when I migrated to the USA, fresh out of high school. I left the comfort and familiarity of my mother's home and native Jamaica, to settle in a new world of uncertainty. I came to Washington, DC with the plan to continue my education here. With only a visitor's visa, I had to figure out the logistics of getting a student visa, and how to pay the tuition/fees for school.

During these early years, American cities were also feeling the effects of the global turmoil of that era. Like much of the developed world, the USA was in the grips of an economic recession. Unemployment was high, and the crime rate in many urban areas, including Washington DC, was off the charts.

Certainly not the ideal environment, or circumstances for a young, Black male to start a family.

My first foray into parenthood was the proverbial baptism by fire. At the time, my girlfriend Laura and I were living in a sparse studio apartment, atop a restaurant in Silver Spring, Maryland. It had two windows. One faced the brick, back-side of the adjacent building (it was so close, we could touch it with a broom stick,) while the other was a court-side seat to the noise and traffic of a busy highway and the idlers who congregated outside the building. Brick wall or traffic/idlers, those were our only outdoor viewing options

Neither Laura nor I was prepared to raise kids, either as parents or as a couple. For me, it was like a head-first dive into uncharted waters and, need I remind you, I couldn't swim. To quote Donald Rumsfeld, the former USA Secretary of Defense: "We did not know what we didn't know." It was this naivete that led us to take the plunge into parenthood. There was no time to think about our commitment to each other, our living arrangements, or even our suitability to be parents.

I was working as a janitor at the time and my salary was just above the minimum wage. Though I had just graduated from college, it was difficult finding a higher paying job in the economic climate of the day. To make matters worse, neither Laura nor I had visas that authorized us to work or live in the USA. As such, our options for a place to live were limited to low-income housing ones, and the concrete jungles of America welcomed us with open arms. This gave us a front row seat to the cat and mouse soap opera featuring the police and drug dealers and petty criminals. With limited options available, our life was one of navigating a path that kept us on track to our career goals and avoided the temptations of "easy money," either from social security fraud or other criminal activities.

The reverberations from the prevailing global unrest would inevitably reach the USA, as exemplified by the second oil crisis of 1979.

It began when the Iranian revolution of 1979 toppled the US backed Shah of Iran, Reza Pahlavi, and elevated Ayatollah Khomeini as supreme leader. Months after, student revolutionaries stormed the US embassy in Tehran and held fifty-two USA diplomats as hostages. This hostage crisis, and a subsequently botched USA rescue attempt, would contribute to President Carter's loss to Ronald Reagan in the 1980, USA presidential election. On the heels of this was the Iran-Iraq war that began in 1980. Oil production in both countries fell drastically and global oil prices increased dramatically, in response. This "oil crisis" triggered a world-wide economic recession. In the USA, the price of a barrel of crude oil more than doubled. The sudden increase in oil prices further exacerbated an already existing USA monetary inflation.

Inflation effectively decreases the purchasing power of any currency. In the USA, monetary policies are geared towards keeping the rate of inflation around 3% annually, to preserve the purchasing power of the dollar.

By 1981, however, inflation had reached 14% in the US (Fed Reserve public data.) In response, the Federal Reserve began a series of interest rate increases to rein in inflation. This monetary policy also had unintended consequences. The Savings and Loans industry (S&L), which depended on low interest rates from the Federal Reserve to make loans to consumers, was mortally wounded. S&Ls went into crisis mode with the subsequent collapse of that segment of the US economy.

The so called "S&L Crisis" precipitated when consumers could no longer afford to take out loans due to the exorbitant interest rates the banks and S&Ls were charging. Mortgage rates rose to 18% and put homeownership beyond the reach of most Americans. As such, there was hardly any activity in the housing sector of the US economy. Another economic recession was underway by 1987 and unemployment went as high as 11%.

On October 19, 1987, stock markets around the world crashed. This led to a major sell-off on US stock exchanges in response. The Dow-Jones Industrial Average, a major stock market index, lost more than twenty percent of its value. The specter of inflation and unemployment loomed.

Lurking behind all this economic turmoil was a rapid increase in crime and violence in urban America, with the largest increases seen on the east coast. This increase in crime was attributed to the introduction of the cheap, highly addictive crack cocaine from South America, into poor, inner-city communities.

Cocaine production in South America saw exponential growth during the 1970s, with Colombia as its epicenter. By the 1980s, it became more profitable for Colombian farmers to cultivate coca leaf, the raw material of cocaine, than coffee or banana. Illegal cocaine created ridiculous profits for the trafficker and spawned brutal crime waves in its wake. The crime wave would inevitably flow to US cities as cocaine's popularity increased here.

Crack-cocaine, a cheaper, more addictive version of cocaine was unheard of before 1985. It made the euphoria and addiction of cocaine accessible to the poor man. By 1990, crack had taken root in urban America and brought along its baggage of addiction, death, and destruction. Murder rates in large USA cities reached record numbers. There was growing outrage in society as Americans came to grips with the disturbing statistics. The politicians whose manifestos included tough, anti-crime policies were the ones winning elections. Their anti-crime policies were mostly punitive and emphasized jail and more jail time. For the many who became addicted to crack, resources for rehabilitation and recovery were few and far between. The Government's addiction prevention campaign during the Reagan presidency was led by First Lady Nancy Reagan. It revolved primarily around their "Just say No!" slogan. If you said "yes," and became addicted to drugs, you were treated like a leper (and a criminal) with limited options for kicking the habit. Your road to recovery would be an epic journey of ridicule, blame, shame, and the possibility of incarceration. For many addicts, it seemed easier to run a marathon while holding their breath than to find sobriety.

This was a tough time for an America that was witnessing the US economy throwing people out of work, and some into the welcoming arms of a crack-cocaine epidemic eager to recruit dealers and users alike. Couple this with the limited rehab options available for drug addicts to get clean, and we got inner-city communities that were forever (negatively) transformed by drugs and violence. Definitely not the place for young, impressionable, Black males to "find" themselves - literally and figuratively.

The combined impact of President Reagan's War on Drugs and President Clinton's Crime Prevention bills created an exponential increase in the number of incarcerated individuals in America. According to a Justice Policy Center report, roughly two prisons per month were being built to accommodate these inmates. The demographics of the prison population were also changing. By the year 2000, the number of Black males that were incarcerated, mostly for drug related offenses, had increased 400%.

Blacks, who make up roughly 13% of the US population, became 40% of the prison population. As a reference, the numbers for whites are 76% and 29%, respectively. The unintended consequence of these "wars," on crime and drugs, was the mass incarceration of Black males. There are now 2.3 million prisoners in USA jails, close to 40% of whom identify as non-Hispanic black.

The reality of these statistics resonated beyond the prison walls. Black children were growing up without fathers and good, male role models. Black household income was also being negatively impacted. Additionally, drug addiction was becoming endemic in many urban communities, bringing its own negative social, political, and economic consequences.

Black families in the 1980s suddenly became the face of everything that was wrong with the USA government social and welfare programs. In fact, Laura and I were to become part of a growing, troubling statistic: the rise in poor, unmarried Black parents depending on the government for support. This demographic was being villainized (incorrectly) in the media as the biggest burden on the country's social services and the driving factor behind the surge in crime and violence in America. Black Americans were blamed for the crack-cocaine epidemic which was spreading along the east coast like wildfire.

So, there we were, two young, unmarried Blacks embarking on first-time parenthood. Me working as a Janitor, she unemployed. The only thing missing from the stereotype was for one (or both) of us to be using or selling crack. Thankfully, neither Laura nor I, had any use for illicit drugs.

Laura's first sonogram confirmed that she was pregnant with twins! Just our luck. Two neophytes in the parental game, and our degree of difficulty suddenly doubled. Thankfully, Laura was way ahead of me on the parenting scale and was a quick study.

We were both doing on-the-job training, but she was doing the majority of the heavy lifting. When Laura gave birth, it was to fraternal twins, Imani (girl) and Daniel (boy.) We quickly realized that they were two different individuals, with their own unique needs: Imani was an extrovert, while Daniel was more introverted. Daniel had to be rocked to sleep and preferred it done by his mom. Imani preferred that I put her to sleep and boy, did she have the vocal cords to make her demands known. Imani could scream and hold the note for so long that Patti Labelle would have been out of breath by then. Imagine how difficult it became when only one parent was home. After my first two days alone with the twins, I had an enormous amount of respect for single mothers the world over. I was never happier to see Laura, so that I could hand off the twins to her.

The first couple years of parenthood were eye opening, to say the least, but we all survived. Three years later, our third child (second daughter) was born in Alberta, Canada.

Long story short: after a return flight from Jamaica, US immigration officials did not want to allow Laura, with her Canadian passport, to re-enter the USA. She had overstayed her time in the country and had to return to Canada. The immigration officer granted Laura one week to sort out her affairs in the USA, after which she had to get the hell out of their country (not his exact words, but that is what it felt like.) At the time, Laura happened to be several months pregnant. I was in dental school and had just started my clinical years. With everything going on at the time, we decided that Laura would head back to Canada with the children. Healthcare would be free for her in Canada. After she gave birth, they would all return to the US. Prior to Laura's departure, and to confirm our commitment to each other, we got married in a small, civil ceremony at the courthouse.

Laura had an uncle, Bryson, who was living in Edmonton, Alberta. He helped lay the groundwork for her return to Canada. Mponya was born later that year and plans for their return began immediately after. We gathered our meager savings and bought airline tickets for Laura and the three kids to come to Baltimore. At the airport in Canada, US immigration officials denied Laura entry into the US. They said that Laura and the children were traveling to the United States to live and would not be returning to Canada. As such, Laura needed a permanent resident visa, which she did not have.

A new plan was quickly devised: I would travel to Edmonton and take Daniel and Imani, both US citizens, home with me. Uncle Bryson would drive Laura and Mponya across the US border to Montana. There was far less scrutiny at US/Canada road borders than you found at airports. Once they were safely on USA soil, the twins and I would take our flight back to the USA.

That was an intense saga that I remember very clearly. We were operating with a very narrow window of opportunity, and everything had to be like clockwork. I would leave school, after clinic on Thursday afternoon and head to Canada, arriving early Friday morning. Laura and Mponya would go with Uncle Bryson to Montana, on Saturday. They would inform me if the trip to Montana was successful. I would then bring the twins back with me on Sunday and be back in dental school on Monday. Sounds simple, right?

That Thursday afternoon, I caught a Northwest Airline flight to Minneapolis, connecting on to Edmonton. The flight from Minneapolis to Edmonton was the last of its kind, until the following Tuesday. If I missed this connecting flight, it would be useless to continue the mission. Imagine how stressful it became when my flight from Baltimore was delayed. Our plane waited close to forty-five minutes on the tarmac. I could not abandon the mission at this point, even if I wanted to. When the flight arrived in Minneapolis, I had to do an all-out sprint to get to the gate of the connecting flight. As I got to the gate, I could see the plane backing away from the gate.

"This was not how the story is supposed to end!" I remembered thinking.

The Northwest ticketing agent saw the grief and despair in my eyes, and she immediately picked up her phone. I was so out of breath; I could not say a word. The next thing I knew, the plane was pulling back up to the gate. The agent took my boarding pass, I gestured my thanks and boarded the plane. The rest is history.

We had a united family once again, and I got to see my precious, new baby, Mponya. Daniel and Imani were overjoyed to see me. I was their "savior," they told me many years later.

The task ahead now was to bring our united family back to the US.

Laura and Uncle Bryson, who is a catholic priest (and was dressed in official, religious regalia) made it across the border to Montana. From there, Laura and Mponya journeyed via Greyhound bus to our home in Silver Spring, Maryland. Joy!

Laura and I shared similar parental philosophies. Our children's health and education were always a priority. Laura was insistent on a diet of organic/natural food for our family. Organic food, we all know, is not cheap. Since we were living hand-to-mouth at the time, it meant that Laura had to do volunteer work at the organic food store to secure the necessary food rations.

No time or expense was spared to ensure that the children got a first-rate education. No compromises there. This meant moving from an under-performing to a higher performing school district.

Laura always designated time for leading spiritual lessons with our kids. It was important for our children to have a strong moral and ethical foundation.

We were both involved in physical activities and thought it important for the children's well-being, also. It was quite easy to integrate the children into our daily exercise routines. If we were going to exercise, the kids would come along and exercised also. They loved being part of what their parents were doing. Sometimes they would be our exercise props. To simulate weights, for example, I would have Daniel or Imani sit on my back while I did push-ups. This was a fun time for them.

When Laura went jogging, they jogged also. When I went to soccer practice, they came along as well. I was playing with a team consisting of mostly Jamaican players and this gave them a close-up view of their Jamaican roots and culture. My son took to soccer easily and looked forward to being at the soccer field with my team-mates. My team-mates loved him and his sisters, and they felt the love in return.

As a Jamaican, I had to be cognizant of the previously described social climate in the Washington, DC area at the time.

Cocaine and its cheap cousin, crack, were pouring into the DC area from New York and Miami. Drug dealers from New York and Philadelphia were also moving into the area and violently claiming turf. Hostile takeovers, so to speak, of local crack distribution networks. Jamaican gangs, or possies, were heavily involved in these activities. Local Jamaican drug dealers, via their established marijuana distribution networks were turning their attention to the more lucrative crack cocaine trade. If you could not find legitimate work, there was a dealer ready to incorporate you into their posse. Even when you found legitimate work, the temptation of drug money was hard to resist. Drug money was, simply put, massive. Naïve, Black youths, especially those fresh out of Jamaica, were easy targets.

With drugs, comes the obligatory violence. If you are dealing drugs and you do not have a gun, you are among the walking dead. Disputes are resolved personally. No police involved. It is your responsibility to protect yourself and your interests. Ignoring that responsibility could lead to sudden death!

When the Jamaican possies moved into this neighborhood, they turned up the crime volume several decibels. For the first time, the Washington/DC metro area was witnessing execution-style murders on an almost weekly basis. Shoot-outs on the streets were common. Facing superior firepower from the possies, The DC police department was forced to upgrade from thirty-eight caliber revolvers to forty-five caliber automatic weapons.

Us Jamaicans did not have to ask who participated in the drug business. Flamboyance and high-profile were the two terms used to describe Jamaican drug dealers. You could tell by the car they drove, the way they dressed, and who they toured with. We all knew who was who. Even my kids were hip to this. I always spoke to them about the dangers of using and dealing drugs, and how to avoid getting caught up and swept away by its allure.

One evening on our way back from the soccer field, I overheard a conversation between Daniel and Imani:

"If Chris is not selling drugs, how come he's driving a Saab?" Imani asked. Nobody could answer that question, because.... who drives a Saab, anyway? While Chris was not dealing drugs, I could tell the kids were becoming wise to their surroundings.

The places where the dealers came to strut their stuff and to profile were the night clubs and the soccer fields.

Having this sort of ringside view to the crack epidemic also carried associated risks. One would not want to be at the soccer field if rival gang members came looking for an adversary to violently settle a dispute. Thankfully, it did not happen around our team, but it happened on more than a few occasions, elsewhere. Our team did not have many drug dealers on our roster, but we still lost a few players and supporters to drug violence and associated incarcerations.

A Channel 7 TV news report back then, featured an undercover expose of an open-air drug market run by Jamaican drug dealers. At a busy intersection littered with adults and children going about their businesses, we saw handshakes morph into money/drugs exchanges between dealers and buyers. That intersection, by the way, was just two blocks from my apartment. I also recognized all the alleged dealers in that expose. In fact, I occasionally chatted with some of those same guys when I saw them on that street corner. The more I thought about it, the more I realized that I too, could have wound up on the 5pm news. That is life in the concrete jungles, however: wrong place, wrong time, wrong outcome!

Despite my proximity to drugs and drug dealers, getting involved in that business was never a consideration. I had lost a close friend to a drug deal gone sour, so I was aware of the downside of the business. The temptation was there, but I was not interested in that life.

When I graduated with my bachelor's degree, I was told by a drug dealer that a bachelor's was not good enough to get on his payroll. He constantly made fun of the fact that I was working for minimum wage, as a janitor, when I could be living large selling drugs.

It is important to understand that I withstood a lifetime of ridicule and temptation from my peers, here and in Jamaica, because I do not drink alcohol or smoke weed (yes, not all Jamaicans smoke weed.) So, I was ok with being teased and ridiculed. Many years later, the dealer got busted by the police and was deported back to Jamaica. His sons have since taken over from where he left off.

Our children, on the other hand, bore witness to some of our important milestones. They were there when I graduated from dental school and when Laura collected her awards from medical school. I still remember Imani crying at my graduation and not knowing why she was crying. She was five years old.

As soon as they were old enough, the kids came to work with me in my practice, becoming paid employees. There is one incident I will always remember:

Imani had just started working and we agreed on a salary of $10 an hour (well above minimum wages, and easy to calculate wages.) By the time her first paycheck was due, she knew exactly how much she had earned, and that money was spent long before the cheque was in her hand. When Imani finally received her cheque, she ran to me with horror and disbelief in her eyes.

"Daddy! I think CJ is cheating me out of my hours." Imani complained.

"Why don't you sit down with CJ (my office manager) and review your cheque," I countered.

Imani learned an important lesson from her discussion with CJ: Uncle Sam gets paid before you get paid, and even little kids are required to pay taxes. I thought it best that she heard that from someone else.

Imani, Daniel and Mponya became interested in careers in healthcare, mostly from their experiences working with Laura and I.

I went to Imani's graduation, in the same hall that hosted Laura's graduation years earlier and shed a few tears of my own.

Imani is now a practicing Oral Surgeon, who now works with me. We got an entirely different reaction from her when she saw her first pay cheque this time around.

Daniel, like his mom, is a Family Practice physician. He credits his time working with me as an assistant, for making medical school much easier to navigate.

Mponya, after initially starting off as an English major, changed career paths to nursing after she became pregnant with her first child. Her familiarity with patient care in my office made this an easy transition. Today, she is a Registered Nurse, working in the emergency room.

My fourth child, Chinyelu (Chiny) was born during my second year of Oral Surgery residency. I was on my emergency room (ER) rotation and thought I knew everything (I did not.) When Laura had that imminent feeling of giving birth and she suggested that we do the delivery at home, I was game. She had three kids before and knew the drill. Here again, I will quote Donald Rumsfeld: "I did not know what I did not know." Thankfully, the delivery was uneventful, and I delivered a healthy baby girl. That delivery has been the highlight of my life!

We took Chiny to the hospital the following day for an office visit with Laura's OB/GYN. Chiny needed a birth certificate and official registration taken care of. Everyone there was surprised to learn that Laura had given birth, and an oral surgery resident did the delivery. Laura even overheard one of the nurses asking if she should call the police. Thankfully, there was no need to, and the story had a happy ending.

Chiny grew up to be an athlete: an incredibly good middle to long distance runner and a better soccer player. She honed her soccer skills playing with the same Jamaican soccer players that Daniel and I played with from back in the days. Yes, there was still a lot of love there for her as well.

Chiny is now a professional soccer player who has played in soccer's holy grail: The World Cup. In 2019, Chiny represented Jamaica at the FIFA Women's World Cup Finals in France. Jamaica made history in 2019 by becoming the first Caribbean country to participate in a FIFA Women's World Cup. Jamaica repeated that feat in 2022 by qualifying for a second Women's World Cup Finals. Yes, Chiny was a member of this team as well.

Our fifth child, Guemana, was the only planned addition to our brood. Laura wanted a fifth child, and I love children. Enough said. After years of trying, we had practically given up on the idea of a fifth child. Then, boom! 2007 was the year.

With fourteen years between our fourth and fifth child, the parenting landscape had shifted significantly. Children today are better informed and educated about their rights, the law, and current trends. They are growing up with smart phones, social media, the internet and google. This has empowered them with knowledge and information that previous generations did not have access to. They can network with friends, strangers, even "experts," at the tap of a keyboard. I have been fact-checked so many times by my children, that I have to fact-check myself before talking to them, sometimes. Now is the first time in the history of humankind where our children know more about the world around them than their parents. We can no longer dictate orders, or bark commands. It must make sense or be relevant to them. I find myself spending more time negotiating with Guemana than I did with my other four children, combined.

Couple this paradigm shift with a divorce, and your job as a parent becomes exponentially more difficult. Today's kids are experts at exploiting this milieu.

"Well, mama lets me do this when I'm at her house," is something I hear all the time.

While I have had to evolve as a parent, I am sticking with the same playbook used to raise her older siblings: priority placed on health and education; sports and physical activities encouraged, and spiritual development mandated. She is in a household where we all try to abide by these principles, and as my mother liked to say, children live what they learn.

Regardless of the social or political changes taking place around us, the formula for raising good children has remained relatively constant. The experts agree that it starts with a foundation of love, caring for your children and being actively involved in their lives. There is also a consensus on parents being good role models and teaching their children proper morals and ethics. These help them make good healthy choices and usually keep kids out of trouble.

Old Jamaicans will tell you *"bend the tree when it young, when it old it wi bruk."* Bend the tree when it is young and pliable, when it gets old it will break if you try to bend it. While this may be true for trees, it also applies to raising children. It is important to start molding their character when they are young before they are old and set in their ways.

Being a parent is a full-time job that requires presence and commitment. It demands our time, diligence, patience, and love. Much like tending to a garden, where, if you plant good seeds and nurture them appropriately, they will likely germinate and bear good fruits. I think that this will happen anywhere. Even if those seeds are planted in the asphalt ghettos we call "Concrete Jungles."

THE CHILDREN

OUR STAR

That's how we roll
For damage control
Play with the hand we hold
You know we'll never fold

When there is a need
We bring action
Not drugs or weed
But family Intervention

You are my one son
Please understand
Can talk to your mom
Or reason with this man

Remember, you're not alone
I too have Y chromosome
Your sisters have your X's
We're always connected

No matter how far
In peace or war
Ol' bruk or fancy car
You are always our star

- Written for my son, Daniel, after a painful break-up with his
  girlfriend. The entire family journeyed to Columbus, Georgia,
  to comfort and support him.

CONGRATULATIONS!

How great and pleasant it is to see
The evolution of our beloved Imani
Navigating life's obstacles gracefully
Strength and resilience of a baobab tree
Strength and grace make a wicked pair
One we admire, the other elicits fear
Like good medicines oft have bad tastes
Lady and surgeon make strange bedmates

You made it work though, kept it real
Hard work and integrity, not sex appeal
Five long years in full combat mode
Defcon delta on your yellow brick road
Led to their water, you wouldn't drink it
Couldn't be bought with cheap trinkets
A great surgeon is not "great", I suppose
If unwilling to get brown stuff on their nose

History will decide the whys and the hows

You went to drink milk, not to count cows
Certificate in hand, there'll be no more grief
Ode to joy, laughter, and comic relief
Soon to be home where you can rest
A comfy foxhole where you'll be your best
Since your birthday I've watched you grow
From child, to woman, to Learned Fellow

- Celebrating the return of my daughter, Imani, after a grueling 5 years of postgraduate studies culminating in certification as an Oral & Maxillofacial Surgeon.

FAREWELL ADDRESS

Greetings, Imani, my pretty
Away from home, Kansas City
One more day and you're done
Say goodbye to the barrel of that gun

It was great, it's been real
Your time now to rest and heal
Yield not to hate or animosity
Put it in the books of posterity

Higher education has its price
Emotional scars and sacrifice
Lost a few child-bearing years
You endured, no more tears

Stay humble, yet be not afraid
They had the handle, you the blade
As you depart from that town
Armor and sword, please lay down

Give praises to the Man above
Come home, enjoy peace and love
Like Dr King, I'll put you on blast:
You're "Free at last! Free at last!"

- Bitter-sweet memories of Imani's graduation from residency in Kansas City, Missouri, after five years away from home

WORDS TO BE WISE

It's your house, you rule
For kids, that is cool
With age they'll complain
Ask for space, looser reins
Dictator you may be
Teens want autonomy
To themselves to be true
Amid stages they go through

To sail their own ship
Free to launch or to slip
Their life, quite simple
Their body, their temple
We won't always agree
Or like everything we see
What to us seem strange
Kids embrace as change

Not important, let it be
See the forest, not the tree
Change happens constantly
Often quite spontaneously
Mysteries, oft to solve

Require beliefs to evolve
Survival means we adapt
Or fall like Absolute Despots

You're a parent not a friend
Draw the line you'll defend
Discipline's what got you here
Experiences you can share
Life's lessons and wisdom
Spoken by an astute tongue
What life taught us to fear
Kids accept as laissez-faire

You may preach even shout
Likely they'll tune you out
Learn they must on their own
Rediscover what is known
Step back let them see
The monster in Reality
Have faith be not afraid
This is how Character's made

Master time will surely tell
If you prepared them well
Fate's surely unpredictable
Disasters are inevitable
Whoever thinks all to know
Life delivers many a blow
Then Wisdom makes us realize
Knowledge doesn't make one wise

- Inspired by my daughter Mponya, after she embarked on her journey of motherhood.

WORLD CUP

I'm here, no mystery
To witness history
My babe all grown up
Off to the World Cup

Backyard to playgrounds
Rec fields, kick-arounds
Bogota, Shymkent
Devoted student
Learnt, grew, and improved
Finally found her groove

Canada, Cuba, Costa Rica
None tougher than Jamaica
Our dream is for real
Victory, ours to steal

Of these Epics they spoke
Time now to go for broke
Though tough as steel
Even Achilles had his heel
Big tree, we're small axe
Our Alamo is in Texas!

- Written after reflection on the long odyssey that brought my daughter, Chinyelu and the Jamaican senior national team, to Edinburg, Texas, for the CONCACAF World Cup qualifiers.

CHILD OF MINE

Oh, child of mine, you're my blessing
Sometimes, though it's quite distressing
Born during a period of great turbulence
Gifted with wit, beauty, and intelligence

Found you worn, in need of renovation
An ongoing task of constant innovation
Finding the formula, setting the right tone
Takes this parent from his comfort zone

Life as a single dad is especially hard
Your kids will play you like the wild card:
"I don't have to do chores at Mama's home"
"She would never confiscate my phone"

Today's children are more empowered
Parenting standards arguably lowered
Diluted by the courts and legislators
Schools, Social workers, administrators

Gone are the days of Dictators, Autocrats
Replaced by Negotiators and Diplomats

Trading access to the phone and internet
To get chores done and our kids' respect

Raising a child now is a constant Barter
Especially if said child is a teen daughter
Do this for me, and I'll do that for you
Experience and wisdom are of no value

It's out with the old, usher in the new
Gigi, my daughter, defending her milieu
Listens to Tupac, Cordae and J Cole
No Reggae, no funk, nor rock and roll

Gigi doesn't like soccer, TT, or Ballet
Loves Cinnabon, beef patties, Chipotle
Came with her dog as a package deal
This minor detail she forgot to reveal

So Mami is here, and I don't know why
A dog without wings who is able to fly
Has flown to Canada, France, Cameroon
Took to the skies to come from Saskatoon

An inside, lap dog who roams the house
A canine ninja, more like a big furry mouse
Stealthily raids the trash bin for food
Then enjoys the spoils in quiet solitude

This is a dog who's not MY best friend
No more time on it I'm willing to spend
Enough on my plate with a girl I adore
About my little girl I'll tell you some more

Gigi goes to games and says she had fun
Without knowing the score, or even who won
Not a sports fan, which should be clear
Unless it's Boxing, where she has no fear

I'll take her to the Mall, but I dare not enter

Not as her parent, nor as her mentor
In my company she's a fish sans water
In Diplomatic terms, I'm "persona non grata"

Privacy she protects better than Fort Knox
Attitude that jars like a car without shocks
Traits I recognize that are totally mine
Payback, I guess, from the Holy Divine

Whatever her flaws, she's still my gal
From day one through Grace Episcopal
One day at a time is how we'll make it
Love you very much, just can't fake it

- Work in progress as single dad raises his last daughter. Her mom filed for divorce while Gigi was in Elementary school (Grace Episcopal Day School.) She later took her to Saskatoon, Canada for middle school. In 2020, Gigi came back to live with me to attend high school and be closer to her siblings.

WORK IS NOT A FOUR-LETTER WORD

"Patient man ride donkey"

I came from very humble beginnings. My mom was a poor country girl, and my father, also from the country, was mostly on the road and in and out of jobs. Our family lived in a modest house in Kingston that my mother inherited from her mother. The house always seemed to need repairs. Especially its zinc roof, which leaked in several places when it rained. It seemed that every room in the house had a bucket and a stack of newspaper for when it rained.

I still remember us cooking dinner on a coal fired stove and bathing in a bucket outside in the backyard. Our family never owned a fridge or tv until I got to primary school. It was the life I knew and enjoyed, and our family considered ourselves well off. There was food on our table, a roof over our heads and we went to the best public schools in Jamaica, based on merit.

In our household, discipline, good manners, and respect were strictly enforced. School work and homework was to be taken seriously. Our uniforms (khaki pants and khaki shirt, in my case) had to be clean and neatly pressed for school. For most of my six years in primary school, I had one set of uniforms that I wore to school. One khaki shirt, one khaki pants, worn five days per week to school. When I got home from school in the afternoons, one of the first things I had to do was wash my uniform and hang them out to dry. It was especially important to do this when the sun was out, so the uniform would be dry and ready for ironing the next morning. Leaving the uniform outside, overnight, was out of the question. It would be pilfered before daylight. Oh yes, I had to have clean, pressed uniforms for school. I was not getting out of my mother's house with wrinkled, or dirty clothes.

Fridays were my favorite day of the week because it meant that I did not need to wash or iron my uniform for school the next day. Washing my uniform was a chore, and like all my other chores, I hated it. Washing, cleaning, sweeping was not for me. "Scarce o' labor," a British phrase for a lazy person, is what my mother used to call me. Work was not supposed to be viewed as a "four letter word."

I came to the United States of America in the summer of 1980, right after graduating high school, on a visitor's visa. My suitcase was a small one and barely half filled. The little "stuff" I had was pilfered, in front of my eyes, by friends and family who rummaged through my suitcase, the day before my departure. They all claimed, and I too believed, that since I was going to the US, I could easily get more, newer, and better "stuff." I was going to the land of plenty. The great USA.

Just getting a US visa stamped in your passport was celebrated in my neighborhood, like you won the Mega Million lottery. You would not need old clothes anymore. Boy was I in for a rude awakening.

The game plan on my arrival to the US was to matriculate into a university and then try to convert my visitor's visa to a student's visa. By September of that year, I was not in school, and my visitor's visa had expired. I was living on a couch, in a two-bedroom apartment, with my sister Jackie, and her family. Even though Jackie and family were very gracious about the accommodation, I felt like a prisoner. I was in a strange country, had no friends, no money, and no means to get around. I desperately wanted to return home to Jamaica, but I could not.

Returning to Jamaica empty-handed would automatically brand you a failure. One could not go to the great USA and return to Jamaica without anything tangible or of value to show for your time there. Those same people who celebrated your visa would now call you worthless and a waste of public funds!

Who leaves Jamaica with nothing and returns home to nothing? Certainly not Kevin Asher. My oversized ego would have no part of that. Failure was not an option.

Now, all I had to do was find a job, save money, and use it to pay for school. Simple enough, right?

Not so simple when you are an illegal alien, with no work permit, and no marketable skills. I was literally and figuratively, "scarce o' labor," personified.

To make matters worse, the unemployment rate in the US at the time was officially ten percent. In reality, it was worse than that. President Reagan had stopped counting people who were not actively looking for work, in the unemployment census.

I remember going to a job interview at The Sheraton Hotel, in Washington, DC. They were hiring housekeepers/janitors. It was my first job interview and there were quite a few people there. I wore a pair of blue jeans and a sky-blue, button-down shirt, I borrowed from Jackie's boyfriend, Bunny. Nothing fancy. Seated beside me, applying for the same job, was a guy wearing a suit and tie and toting a briefcase.

Damn right! I did not get that job, or any of the other jobs I applied for.

Eventually, it became time to tap into the network of the illegal alien community, where you could source "off the Immigration and Naturalization Service (INS) radar" jobs. Via that same network, and for the right price, one could buy US birth certificates, social security numbers, fake green cards, etc. (I could not afford, nor considered, those options.)

Through a friend of a friend, I got a job house cleaning in a private home. Newton, a Jamaican, was in his junior year of college and needed to buckle down, and pass Mathematics 101, a class he was forced to drop twice. He had two jobs and felt the need to let go of one. Fortunately, both stories had happy endings: I got the job and Newton passed his math class.

By now the irony should be apparent: scarce o' labor (me) who hated doing chores, now desperate for a job doing chores (aka, housekeeping.) Talk about being forced to confront your demons.

I worked for a family of Russian immigrants, who lived in Georgetown. He, a lawyer; she, a pediatrician working at Georgetown University Hospital. They understood my situation and made me feel extremely comfortable. I worked in their home, on the weekends, for a couple of years. It was obvious though, that if I wanted to save for college, I would need another job.

In steps Newton again. Newton was working as a Janitor, at the luxurious Forum Condominiums, in Rockville, Maryland. Based on his recommendation, I was hired as a Janitor at the Forum. It was my first "official" job in the US and was a job I grew to love. I could save for college, the days were flexible, and there was enough downtime to study. There were other, less tangible, but important benefits, though. The Forum Condominiums is a 352 unit building with residents from various parts of the world and walks of life. There was much to learn about the USA and the world, from my interactions with the residents. The residents also provided a steady stream of discarded journals, and newspapers which I used to broaden and diversify my knowledge base. I met and befriended a lot of interesting characters at the Forum.

Despite my status on the Forum's social totem pole, I interacted with the residents as their equal. I refused to be intimidated by their status or wealth. I was brought up by a mother who taught me to treat my fellow men (rich or poor) with dignity and respect.

"We are all equal under the eyes of the Lord," she used to say.

I also make it a habit to decline monetary tips, or rewards, for minor assistance I offer to anyone. If it falls under the definition of "common courtesy," I will respectfully, but firmly, decline the tip. I cannot tell you how many times I have had to run away from Forum residents, chasing me to stuff money in my pockets. Helping someone bring their groceries, for example, up to their apartment is not worthy of a tip. Hell no; thank you - I also tried to be polite.

Even to the cigarette puffing witch (spelled with a "B") who terrorized and yelled at the receptionists and janitorial staff, at every opportunity. She could always expect a polite, respectful greeting whenever our paths crossed. No, we never became best buddies. No happy ending there. I respected her and she respected the fact that I respected her and was not intimidated by her antics.

Then there was the Polish Jew/World War II survivor, Izzy. He came to the US after World War II and struck it rich as a furrier in New York City. We would speak at length about his youthful days in Poland and how the rough times there prepared him to survive a WW II Nazi concentration camp. Izzy always drove the fanciest car that Cadillac made. Said he would never, under any circumstances, buy a German or Japanese car. Not hard to figure out why.

I used to talk about politics with the very distinguished, well dressed, Black lady, Ms. Harper. She told me that she used to write speeches for the first President Bush. It was from my conversations with her, that I learned that Presidents, most times, do not write their own speeches. I was also impressed that President Bush had a Black woman writing his speeches.

The Forum was a great place to work. Our boss, Ms. Alspaugh, was a sweetheart and I worked with a great group of guys. For the entire time I worked at the Forum, nobody got fired.

My coworkers were Newton, until he graduated from college; Wayne, an African American, my age; Tamba Yamba, from Sierra Leone; and Joseph, a Haitian immigrant.

Wayne was the only US citizen on the janitorial staff. He, probably, was the only one of us legally authorized to work in the country. I did not know Joseph very well, because he worked the morning shifts. He was also much older than us and was usually gone well before I arrived for my evening shifts. His English was not that great either, so there was not much to talk about during our brief encounters.

I knew for sure, though, that neither I, Newton nor Tamba had legal papers to be in the US, let alone work in the US. I suspect that Ms. Alspaugh also knew we were undocumented and not authorized to work. You could say that there was a "don't ask, don't tell" policy in effect at the Forum: she did not ask, we did not tell.

Tamba was an experienced janitor and had been working at the Forum way before I got there. I was shocked when I found out that he had a Master of Business Administration (MBA) degree, from a prestigious US university, under his belt. Time Magazine ran a cover story, during this time, anointing the MBA "The Most Coveted Degree in America." His immigration status was the only thing preventing him from capitalizing on that investment. Tamba, a few years older than Newton and me, was one of the nicest people I have met in my life. He was kind, modest, soft spoken, and humble. You could tell from the way he carried himself, that he came from a noble upbringing. Tamba's lunch always became "our" lunch. He was the only one of us who owned a car, and if you worked his shift, you would get a ride home. You could not refuse. If there was a foot of snow on the ground, you would still get a ride home. If you needed someone to cover for you, Tamba was there. "No" was the most difficult word to find in his vocabulary. He was a nice guy to a fault.

Tamba was the only one of us actively trying to legitimize his status. Newton and I heeded the word in the illegal alien community: if you do not notify the INS of your status, they won't know that you are in the country illegally. We did not meet the criteria for change of status, anyway, so we did not bother.

It was a semi-depressing state of being for the three of us: full of dreams, hopes, aspirations, and university educated (in the land of opportunity,) but corralled and restrained by our undocumented status. To make matters worse, at any time we could be deported back to our native countries if the INS found out about our status. Whereas Tamba sought to change his status, Newton and I were like two "Jack-in-the box," waiting patiently and quietly for someone, or something, to press the buttons so we could pop out and soar to the heights we dreamed of.

One fateful night, Tamba and I were on duty at the Forum. We were both tasked with stripping and refinishing the lobby's marble floor. It was a job that took several hours of work. Tamba told me to take my break early, so we could complete the job before our shift ended. I always took my break, about thirty minutes long, away from the comings and goings of the Forum, so I could mentally recharge.

When I returned from my break that evening, the lobby was a scene of total chaos: the buffing machine was discarded in the middle of the lobby's floor, with the electrical extension cords strewn all over the place. The lobby furniture and area rugs were thrown about indiscriminately. The place looked like the aftermath of a flash tornado.

I found out later that agents from the INS had come to detain Tamba, while I was away on break. Tamba was taken immediately to an INS detention center, from where he was deported, two days later, to his native Sierra Leone.

There is no doubt in my mind that if I were there with Tamba, I too, would have been detained by the INS agents, and summarily deported. No doubt whatsoever. This was a scary reminder of my status as an illegal alien living in the United States and how fickle my existence in the country could be. For several weeks thereafter, I spent many sleepless nights debating the pros and cons of staying in the US. I didn't want to be the next Tamba.

For Tamba, this was truly a sad ending to an immigration drama, starring a benevolent and decent human being. I never heard from Tamba again. My efforts to find him have, so far, been futile.

Ironically, about one year after Tamba's deportation, the Immigration Reform and Control Act was signed into law by President Ronald Reagan. It granted amnesty to millions of illegal aliens living in the US, and a pathway to US citizenship. Had he not been deported, Tamba would have met the criteria to become a legal, permanent resident in the US.

I often think about Tamba Yamba and wonder how things turned out for him. Sierra Leone experienced an atrocious civil war, from 1991 to 2002, that resulted in roughly seventy thousand deaths, 2.6 million displaced citizens and unspeakable crimes against humanity. Was fate kind to Tamba during those eleven years of terror, I often wonder.

Newton and I used that same law to legalize our status. For both of us, that journey to legal status was full of fits and starts, that required a lot of patience and faith. I often compared this journey to a jackass ride. A jackass, or donkey, is notorious for being a very stubborn animal. As the Jamaican saying goes, *"takes a patient man to ride a donkey,"* and our patience paid off when we rode our way to legal US citizenship.

The United States of America is one of the few places on earth where janitors can move on to bigger and better things. Hard work, discipline, and a little luck can take you far. Wayne's brother, John, became a star player for the Atlanta Hawks and Cleveland Cavaliers, in the NBA. John bought a multi-unit apartment building in Washington, DC, that Wayne moved on to manage.

Newton went to law school and, last time I heard, was working in the District Attorney's office in Cleveland, Ohio.

I left the Forum after obtaining my undergraduate diploma. Two years after, I enrolled in dental school, later specializing as an oral and maxillofacial surgeon.

Every so often, I would drive past the Forum, on Rockville Pike, and reminisce on those formatives, "donkey" years and the dreams we had.

I also think about all the other people who have touched my life in a positive way and helped nurture me to where I am today. I realize that I have a great many people to thank. That list of people starts with my mother and there are so many names on it, I never get to the end. That is because my thought takes me further back in time: to a naked, young boy blissfully splashing water on himself in a metal bath pan, outside, in a Jamaican backyard. Laughter fills the air. That same boy is seen later romping gleefully with his younger brother. Both are half naked and bare-footed, in the rain. They are now being yelled at by their mother, who knows her son's shenanigans will give his younger brother a cold. She is terribly upset, because she will have to miss work the next day, to care for her ailing, asthmatic son.

"Kevin!" A voice interrupts. "What's going on? Why are you crying?"

As I am yanked back into the realm of the present, there are tears streaming down my cheeks. I scan the office and notice that a bunch of bemused eyes are all pointed at me. None quite sure what to make of the moment.

I needed a moment to reflect on my youthful days, underlined by joy filled poverty, to where I now sit in my office as a specialist in oral and maxillofacial surgery. Quite an odyssey for a poor country boy, and one hell of a jackass ride.

Today, over thirty years after last working at the Forum, is supposed to be a happy day. No tears allowed. I am in my office with a real estate agent and a settlement attorney. I am getting ready to sign the deed for my new home. The address:

11801 Rockville Pike
Apt #333
Rockville, MD 20852
The Forum Condominiums.

THE NUCLEAR COLONY

"Nuh throw 'way yu stick before yu cross di water"

Have you ever wondered what life would be like after a nuclear holocaust? Where and how would you live thereafter? Would it make sense to form colonies or cooperatives with other survivors to improve long-term chances of survival? The fallout shelters, designed to weather the aftermath of a nuclear attack, do they have capacity limits? Who would you want in your nuclear shelter or colony?

That last question was a real one I had to ask, at one of the most desperate and depressing junctures in my life.

A significant portion of my childhood was spent butting heads with my mother. My father was mostly on the road for work and chose not to exercise his parenting skills when he was home. My mother did all the parental heavy lifting in our household, and she was a strict disciplinarian.

I was a rebel. I rebelled against the strict discipline my mother imposed on us children - the regular chores, the curfews, censorship of the friends we could keep, the clothes we wore, language we spoke, where we went, etc. My mother even insisted that we speak proper English in her presence. This in Jamaica, land of wood, water, and patois (the local dialect.)

A rebel and a disciplinarian can't live under the same roof. Period! I concluded. One of us had to go and the disciplinarian's name was on the title of the house.

"As soon as I'm done with school, I'm moving out. Can't take this foolishness anymore!" I would declare, whenever I argued with my mother.

I could not wait for my eighteenth birthday. Then I would be done with school, get a job, move out of my mother's house and be free to do as I pleased.

As my high-school graduation approached, the theme song from the movie, "Mahogany," was the number one song on the Jamaican musical charts. It was sung by Diana Ross, who starred in the movie along with Billy "Dee" Williams - the two great performers of the era, in their respective genres. Everyone loved the movie and its theme song. I couldn't stand it!

The chorus of the song was a constant, nagging reminder of my shortcomings and my fear of what the future held. Where would I live? How would I get a job? Questions like these would reverberate in my head whenever I heard the song -

"Do you know where you're heading to?
Will you like the place that your life is taking you?
Do you ...?"

Diana Ross bossed that chorus with her distinctive, melodic voice. I had no idea where I was going, or what I would be doing, so the song served as an anxiety trigger. As the number one song of the day, it was always on the air, feeding my growing anxiety.

I soon became aware that a job doesn't magically appear in your lap when you turn eighteen years old. More so when you don't have any tangible, marketable skills. Reality didn't pull any punches either, when I found out the cost of renting an apartment or even a room in a tenement yard. I had to swallow my pride and beg my mother to stay in her house. I understood exactly why my older siblings were still living at home. A wise Jamaican saying came to mind: "nuh throw 'way yu stick before yu cross di water." Never throw away your stick before you cross the water.

Years later, when I was fresh out of university, with papers in hand, I went on the prowl in search of employment. I had just graduated with honors from the prestigious Howard University, in the nation's capital, and I assumed that finding a job would be easy. Anticipating a higher paying job, I had moved out of my sister's apartment just before graduation. Once more, "throwing away my stick before crossing the water!"

After twenty-odd interviews, miles of walking and a covert takedown of my self-confidence, I was forced to revisit the reality of what no tangible, marketable skill meant. This time though, there was no mama to provide a safety net. With an undergraduate degree in microbiology, it became clear that I was qualified to do absolutely nothing!

On my job interviews I kept hearing the same thing:

Them: "Do you have any experience? "

Me: "No."

Them: "The position requires experience."

Me: "But I need a job to get experience."

Them: "We'll call you." (HR code phrase for "We have no more time to waste on you!")

It felt like I was living a literal "chicken or the egg" joke: which came first, the job or the experience?

The answer, in my case, was irrelevant since I didn't have either.

I remember applying for a research job working directly with the HTLV virus. HTLV underwent a name change to HIV a year later. Back in the days, the virus we now know as HIV generated the same hype as Ebola does today. Nobody wanted to work with that virus. No (expletive deleted) body! If you got infected by it, death was guaranteed in less than five years. There was no cure. If your doctor diagnosed you with HTLV, the best he could do was give you a prescription for a shovel.

That should give you an idea of how desperate I was, however, for a job. A real job. Not the janitors' job I had at the Forum condominium. It was time now for a decent salary, a reliable car, a move out of the 'hood, and financial independence.

Well, guess what? I didn't get that job either.

If I couldn't get a job that nobody wanted, then obviously I needed to try something else. A new approach perhaps.

That new approach came via the advice of a prominent Jamaican drug dealer who played on my soccer team. He brought clarity to my dilemma:

"Wha yuh going do with a bachelor's degree?" He asked. "Yuh not even qualified to get a job with me. Yuh need advanced education to be on my payroll," he continued. Then, in the most eloquent English, he quoted from Alexander Pope's "Essay on Criticism," that many of us learned in high school:

"A little learning is a dangerous thing.
Drink deep or taste not the Pierian Spring.
There, shallow drinks intoxicate the brain.
While drinking largely sobers us again..."

I was left stunned by his command of English literature, while he and his posse had a good laugh at my expense. Despite his profession, he was a wise elder who was good at dispensing timely, useful advice (most times.)

Four hard grueling years of playing by the rules and it took a drug dealer to show me the light. Not only that, but he also spoke in proper English. It seemed as if mama was speaking to me directly.

I agreed. I needed "advanced education." Not the drug dealing kind though, but from an accredited university.

As I pondered my next move, I used the following search criteria to select my area of advanced study: if there is a nuclear holocaust tomorrow and there is only one spot left in the colony, who gets in?

It was an appropriate question to ask since the Cold War between the US and the USSR was still in full swing. With all the saber rattling going on then, a nuclear holocaust was a possibility, and many of the nuclear fallout shelters have posted capacity limits.

I finally settled on studying dentistry. I chose to pursue dentistry as a career for several reasons. First off, I liked the field of healthcare and had fulfilled all the prerequisites for dental school via my microbiology degree. It would be an easy transition. I was also very good at working with my hands. Dentists do make a decent salary and graduate with the tangible, marketable skills necessary to start working without supervision.

I was fortunate enough to get into the University of Maryland Dental School. They had a combined DDS/PhD program that put them at the top of my dental school list. It was a very competitive program where students would complete their dental degree in four years and the PhD within two additional years (six years total.) It also came with a stipend. Two degrees for the price of one, plus money? Sign me up. Please!

Dental school is very demanding mentally, emotionally, and physically. It's an all hands on deck deal. Throwing concurrent PhD studies onto that deck could easily sink one's dental school career. I had spent the past four years working three jobs, while being a full-time student. I had no doubts about my ability to complete both degrees successfully and convinced the professors to allow me into the combined degree program.

After my second year in dental school, I thought it best to go as far as I could in my chosen profession via specialty training. That quote from Alexander Pope was still echoing in my subconscious. I had to "Drink deep."

Dentistry had ten recognized specialties to choose from, but oral and maxillofacial surgery (OMS) was the only one that paid its residents a stipend. OMS was, therefore, the only specialty I could afford to pursue. I had a wife and two children at the time, and we could not afford to take on any more debt.

There would be some logistic obstacles to overcome, however. The American Dental Association limits the number of residency slots available each year. As one of the most competitive specialties, OMS programs usually choose from the top two students of each graduating class. I was neither the number one nor the number two ranked student in my class. In fact, you would have to travel quite a distance down my class ranking to find my name. In a class of one hundred thirty, finding me on that list was like looking for Carmen San Diego.

Class rank was the solid, intimidating brick wall standing between me and OMS residency. I now had two more years of dental school to climb up the class ranks and to improve my resume.

My last two years of dental school were the clinical years, and this was where I excelled. Still smarting from my job application debacle, I decided to volunteer in an oral surgery office to get more "experience."

My wife and I called all the oral surgery practices listed in the phone book (there was no google back then) to enquire if I could volunteer in their office. In the entire Washington DC metropolitan area, only one surgeon, Dr. Leonard Goldman, agreed to accommodate me. He had one condition though: he would only bring me on as an employee. As he rightly explained:

"If you come to volunteer, you will show up once in a while. If I pay you to work, you will never miss a day."

Every Saturday from junior year to graduation, I was in his office. He was a wonderful surgeon, great mentor, and obligingly wrote one of my OMS letters of recommendation.

By the time applications were due for residencies, I had not cracked the top ten of our class rank. I was trending upwards, but still unsure of my ability to get into an OMS residency. The only way to know for sure was to apply. So, I packed up all my dental school achievements, transcripts, oral surgery and research experience, letters of recommendation, removed my tail from between my legs, and submitted my applications.

Much to my surprise (and delight,) I was invited for interviews by four programs. The research experience from the PhD component of my studies was a big asset, I was told. My uncertainty was later transformed to opportunity when I matched to Howard University's OMS program. They wanted someone who could hit the ground running and my oral surgery work experience weighed favorably on my behalf.

Once I started OMS residency, it was readily apparent that its long, unpredictable hours would not allow me to continue with the PhD. I had managed to complete the required classes but was nowhere close to finishing the research. I had done enough work, though, to earn a Master of Science in Physiology for my efforts.

After four years of residency, I received my certificate in oral and maxillofacial surgery. This time around, there was no anxiety. I didn't even need to apply for a job, because I had a job offer prior to graduation. The job interview was a mere formality. Since then, a lot of job recruiters have come knocking on my door.

I realize that a profession in healthcare is not for everyone. Not everybody wants to deal with blood, gore, and bodily fluids, or even people, on a daily basis. Regardless of the career path you choose, there are common themes that apply across all careers:

It is easier to get a job when you have a tangible, marketable skill, so I recommend that you choose wisely what you study.

Experience is a great asset to have going into any job interview. If you must volunteer to get it, find the time to volunteer.

Success does not always come from chasing the bag. When you work honestly and diligently perfecting your craft, the bag often comes looking for you. There is always a market for excellence in any career field.

Knowledge and education are the currencies of today's meritocratic world. The more you have, the wealthier you become, literally and figuratively. I got my job, not because of who I am, my race, or creed, but primarily, because of what I know.

Choosing to study OMS was a wise decision for me. During the recent Covid shutdown of the US economy, when millions of workers were laid off, our office stayed open for business. In fact, it was a very busy time for my practice. The Covid 19 pandemic has been the closest thing to a nuclear holocaust that mankind has witnessed in my lifetime. There were many skilled professionals that helped society weather the lockdown. Teaching, agriculture, food processing, transportation, law enforcement and healthcare were among the essential services that stayed open. After that experience, I feel comfortable that there will be a spot available for a dentist/oral surgeon in any future nuclear colony. Hope we never get to that point, but just in case, my instruments are ready.

ITS A JUNGLE OUT THERE

Trust no shadow after dark

Several decades ago I felt a Divine force, dragging on my shirt collar and leading me to the United States of America(USA). Full of naivety and enchanted by the luster of the great USA, I followed that force. After I graduated from high-school, I arrived in the USA on a visitor's visa, with literally, the clothes on my back and US $80 in my pants pockets. The only things of substance I brought was not in my suitcase, because it was in my head: an outstanding high school education, a passionate belief in myself, and the desire to succeed. "Pig headed" is what many called me.

Migrating to the USA was a huge leap of faith on my part. Though I entered the country on a visitor's visa, I had no intention of returning to Jamaica without a college degree. A very bold declaration to make, especially when I was unsure of my accommodations, had no money for school, no friends in the USA, and didn't know my way around town. I did, however, have my soccer boots, and the notion that together with what I learned in high-school, I could parlay both into a college soccer scholarship.

I also had a sister living in the USA who agreed to accommodate me while I sorted out school. It was a huge sacrifice for her, because my sister, Jackie, was living with her boyfriend and 2 small children in one of the most unpretentious ghettos on the outskirts of Washington DC. It was a community of two-story brick, block shaped buildings, decorated with a couple rows of generic white windows and a door in the middle. As basic as it gets - no awnings, no foyer, no fancy name, no bells, or whistles, with multiple units stuffed unto the lots. You needed a key to get past the building's entrance door, and the apartment door had 3 separate locks. A good indicator of how safe the neighborhood was, but on par for any concrete jungle. This was a low-income rental complex that featured mostly government subsidized families. While the majority of people who lived in the community were decent hardworking citizens, the neighborhood was notorious for its high crime rate, and led the county in the number of murders.

This was my introduction to the USA. I spent most of my early days here indoors and watching TV. I was cautioned against going out alone, especially at night. There was a murder committed 2 blocks away a couple nights before I arrived, so the community was on edge. My sister used the opportunity to remind me of an old Jamaican saying our mother used to tell, for us to negotiate the concrete jungles of Jamaica: "trust no shadow after dark." Meaning, to exercise caution in times and circumstances of uncertainty.

When nothing interesting was on TV, I would peer outside the apartment windows into a dirt and grass playground/courtyard where teenagers and young men would congregate in the afternoons. The gathering spot was under a large gazebo, where the guys came to flex and the girls to strut their stuff. They made a lot of noise - the music, spirited banter, chatter, and the occasional fights. Though it was a playground, I rarely saw any real kids there.

The activity under the gazebo would continue well into the night. The nocturnal crowd, however, would be a more mature group where alcohol and drugs were routinely displayed. The fights and police raids did nothing to deter this crowd, even when gunfire was involved.

I was not too intimidated by all the hullabaloo or those alpha males at the playground. This all reminded me of the Maxfield Park ghetto I used to frequent in Jamaica. I also found out that a few of the guys under that gazebo were Jamaicans. Being a Jamaican myself, I was thus offered a layer of insulation and protection. I knew instinctively, however, this was not a crowd for me to become a part of. Hanging out, hooking up, getting high, or selling drugs was not exactly my idea of having fun. Especially after I heard them bragging about their escapades. I remember one guy, still in high-school, describe how easy it was to rob drunk old men on paydays by waiting for them outside the bar.

I would interact with these guys almost daily as I used the playground to practice soccer (in preparation for that soccer scholarship.) Sometimes I would stop for a minute or two to exchange pleasantries with the Jamaicans. No loitering though.

One afternoon after my workout, on my way back to my apartment, I was confronted by a girl in the group who announced, for all to hear, that she wanted to sleep with me (not her exact words.) She then walked up close to me and lifted up her shirt (nipples at attention) to drive home her point (no pun intended.) This caught me by surprise and shocked me into a visibly paler version of myself. All I could do was offer a nervous smile and keep walking. We had been eying each other for a while, but this brazen, unexpected move was definitely too aggressive for my comfort.

"Super aggressive females" was never a topic of conversations with the guys on my street corner in Jamaica. Definitely not with my mother either. I have four older sisters who were brought up in the school of self-respect and dignity, and I was taught how to appreciate those "lady-like" qualities. I was not used to this type of public solicitation by a girl where the hunter became the hunted.

While I was left adrift in uncharted waters, the group under the Gazebo was dying of laughter. I also got the feeling that this was not the first time something like this happened here, and I wanted no part of that girl after that. Just as well. I later found out that my "flasher" was only 15 years old. Had I yielded to temptation, I could have easily wound up on the Registered Sex Offenders list. Self-discipline and respect, I then realized, are important for survival anywhere, especially in the concrete jungle.

Here I was thinking that it was the guys I had to be weary of. I remember that incident as if it happened yesterday and I grew to appreciate that life in these communities requires constant vigilance. You expect the unexpected, and *you trust no shadow after dark.*

About a month later, to get a break from the mundane and separate myself from that incident, I traveled by bus to New York to visit my good friend, George. He had just migrated from Jamaica. It was my first trip to New York, the mother of all concrete jungles, and I was all starry-eyed when I got there. The skyscrapers, the soulless row houses, the traffic, the noise, littered streets, the smell and the hustle and bustle of people. Lots of people. None of whom smiled or made eye contact. I took a deep breath and inhaled the America I had seen on my tv in Jamaica. Finally, I was in the land of opportunity that I dreamed of!

George was living with his uncle, Roy, in New York. Roy used to be a soldier in the Jamaican army before he came to the USA and remembered me fondly. Somehow, George forgot to tell me that his uncle Roy had a career change and was now a drug dealer. So there I was for 5 days, all the while on pins and needles, living inside a drug "gates" in New York. At any time, the police could raid and I would be thrown in jail for a crime of ignorance (because I was a fool to stay.) Yet another disappointment with the mythical "American dream" and the land of opportunity. Roy even had business cards that he handed out to strangers to solicit customers! This was a definitely a WTF moment for me. What if one of those strangers is a police officer?

"This is how da business works in New York, " he assured me. "Everything cool mon," he continued.

My gut was yelling at me to immediately leave, but Roy was paying for my return ticket home; plus I did not want to look like a punk. Pride and a broke pocket convinced me to ride this one out. A wise man once said, "Fools rush in where angels fear to tread." Yes I was a (expletive deleted) fool! In fact, those infamous "four out of five dentists" would agree that I was a fool.

The front door to Roy's apartment had just as many locks as my sister's, but additionally had a built-in slot for a restraining bar that was used to prevent anyone from forcefully breaking down the door. Yes, definitely not a safe neighborhood. This was confirmed with the stories I heard about murders, gang violence, robberies, etc. Getting robbed in the Bronx, from what I gathered, seemed like a rite of passage.

Then there were the drugs. Lots of drugs. So many people knocking on the door at all hours of the day, that Roy and George worked in shifts. The clientele ranged from the occasional users to the addicts. You could tell who the addicts were based on how often they bought and the currency they used. Addiction brought people of all size, color, and shape to Roy's front door. Some of these people would exchange anything, repeat – anything, for drugs: jewelry, watches, appliances, radios, and yes, sex. In the five days that I was at Roy's house, four different girls offered up their bodies in exchange for drugs. Here again, I punted. Roy and George would make fun of me and question my masculinity when I rebuffed those indecent proposals.

Since George did not have a license at the time, I had to drive his uncle's car to run household errands while he manned the "gates." I relished any opportunity to get out of that apartment. That was until George told me, on my last day there, that his uncle used the car to dump a body a few weeks before my visit.

"Two Puerto Ricans tried to jump my uncle and he had to use his gun to defend himself," George confessed. "One died, the other escaped." Uncle Roy was out on probation from an earlier drug conviction...you can figure it out from there.

"The Puerto Rican who escaped could be hunting this car at any moment, and I could be the revenge trophy," I thought. I never felt safe in that place my entire time in the Bronx. When I boarded the bus to leave New York, and finally made it home, I felt like I had survived the Blair Witch Project.

I would later thank my lucky stars that I resisted the temptation of those ladies bartering sex for drugs. Back then, I was too naïve and ignorant to know the correlation between drug addiction and incurable sexually transmitted diseases like HIV, hepatitis, and herpes. It was my upbringing and intuition that told me, sex for drugs was not a wise exchange. Call it altruism if you will, but I punted, and I'm glad I punted. The peace of mind I have now, because I never waded into those muddy waters, is worth all the ridicule and teasing you can give me.

Self-restraint, respect and *trust no shadow after dark.*

I often visited my in-laws in Cameroon, West Africa. They lived on a farm in a remote village in the jungle. Yes, a real jungle: lions, monkeys, elephants, snakes, the works. A narrow dirt road two hours away from civilization took us to the village. That same road would moonlight as a river bed whenever it rained, so was impassable during the rainy season. You would be literally cut off from civilization for about 3 months every year.

Most of the houses in the village were made with mud blocks and thatched roofs. Their "door" was typically a cloth curtain draped across the entrance. If there is a house with a door in the village guaranteed, it has no lock.

My father in-law moved back to Cameroon after studying in America, so he built a brick house with a metal roof and yes, no locks.

I must admit that it took some time for me to settle and get comfortable on that farm. Dozens of brightly colored lizards soaking up sun in the cleared areas in and around the house. Snakes under just about anything stationary. Geckos on the bedroom walls. The frogs, monkeys, birds crickets and whatever else made a cameo in the night-time choir. Not to mention the mosquitoes always eager to sample foreign blood. Indeed, it took a while.

Then, an old mosquito net provided me with the undisturbed chance to observe the coordinated chaos unfolding around me.

The villagers ate what they caught or grew. The lizards ate the insects; the snakes ate the rats and the lizards; and the geckos love mosquitoes. As I watched the geckos stealthily clean the mosquitoes from the bedroom walls, the ecological order and symbiosis of life in the jungle became apparent. Even the weird noises from deep in the bushes made sense now, and I felt safe.

The irony of me feeling safer in a "real" jungle in Africa, than in America's concrete jungles was not lost. No home invasions, no addicts or psychopaths, no indiscriminate killings. Armed robberies unheard of.

There, the nocturnal and diurnal animals shared the daily playing field and you knew what to expect from both teams. You respect their boundaries; they leave you alone. Self-discipline and respect are important here too, and of course, you trust no shadow after dark.

The subsistence lifestyle of the village demands hard work. Honesty, respect, integrity are endemic, and the wisdom of age is honored and revered. Wisdom is what keeps humans at the top of the food chain in this jungle. There is a soothing, predictable rhythm to this pastoral existence.

I now understood why my in-laws traded in their American jungle, for the one in Cameroon. I too have been thinking about trading in my American jungle.

I have often said that the USA will not be my final resting place, repeating this mantra so many times, that my children are tired of hearing it. They are likely just as tired of hearing me declare that the greatest asset they will inherit from me is wisdom, and once that transfer is done, I can go back home to Jamaica.

With my youngest child heading to college in a few months, it means that all my children will be university educated. Throw in the decades of indoctrination they got from me, and those "four out of five dentists" will agree that I've delivered on that promise. The seeds I planted in America's concrete jungle have now germinated.

My profession as an oral and maxillofacial surgeon has enabled me to transplant my family from the concrete jungle of the USA to the more sedate suburbia. Yet, I have never felt comfortable, or at peace there. Every time I visit my native Jamaica, it gets harder to return to the USA. Family, friends, the beaches, food, the people, the school kids hungry for wisdom and guidance, and the vibrant culture, are all beckoning.

Once again I am feeling that Divine pull. This time, the trajectory is away from the USA, and in the direction of Jamaica. Armed with years of wisdom, tempered with experience, I will make my return soon. As it was several decades ago, the most important assets I will take to Jamaica will be in my head: years of wisdom, understanding, and the failures I learned from.

I well understand that the Jamaica I will return to is not the one I left many years ago. It has its own share of crime and violence, and its own unique concrete jungles. It is also a beautiful country full of wonderful people, the overwhelming majority of whom are decent, God-fearing, law-abiding citizens.

The lessons I learned in the jungles of the USA and Africa are not lost, but it will be important for me to embrace my people and rediscover my country. Getting to know my new neighbors, exploring the country, and reintegrating into the social fabric of Jamaica. Faith, trust, and vulnerability comes along with this. I am prepared for that. Self-discipline and respect applies here as well, and I will still be weary of those to "shadows after dark." Everywhere that I've been to has its own unique "jungle" and dark spaces. Jamaica is the place I call home, where I know and recognize most of the shadows.

POEMS & ESSAYS

Angaza*

Where the sum of our clockwise moments = the sum of our anti-clockwise moments

*Enlightenment in Swahili

SOCIAL COMMENTARY

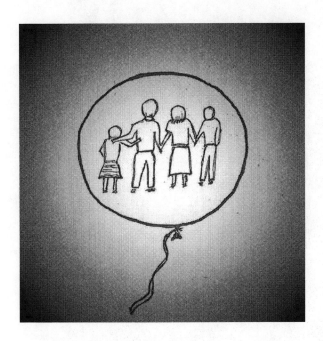

CULTURE CANCELED

Changing of the guard past to present
Person in charge may be an adolescent
Relying on Google to run the kingdom
No experience of age, nor wisdom
Kids telling adults how we should live
What to forget and who to forgive
They'll cite acts from way back when
And cancel for things done at age ten
The Culture of Cancel and being Woke
Served to America like a "pig in a poke"
"A little learning is a dangerous thing"
Long ago written, has a poignant ring

If we scrutinize our high school days
Punctuated with inappropriate displays

Sophomoric behavior blamed on age
Will now elicit protests and outrage
Nobody tells jokes, it's unsafe to laugh
Sense of humor is on a skeleton staff
Life shouldn't be this zero-sum game
Losers condemned to a life of shame
Not even kids get the benefit of a doubt
Now it's one strike and then you're out

Watch what you say, you might be heard
Social media records your every word
Lives and careers razed and disposed
If offensive behavior is diagnosed
No second opinion or informed consent
Cancel culture does not allow dissent
Opinions are debatable until they're facts
Shouldn't be grounds for personal attacks
An offense to you, may not be to me
Even best friends don't always agree

Seems the walls have ears and bushes eyes
Friends and neighbors amongst the spies
Our lifestyle and culture are facing a threat
(Think I should whisper this under my breath)
Independent ideas were once sanctified
To express them now, You'd better hide
I'll stick my neck out and give my opinion:
This only happened in the Soviet Union

The pen, once mightier than the sword
Now usurped by the faceless keyboard
Freedom of speech is a thing of the past
A constitutional favorite is now an outcast
The enemy is here, and it is home-grown
Snooping our mail, computers, and phones
Creating a specter of shame and erasure
For offenses new and old in cancel culture
We once feared monsters, bullies, and robbers
Now the villains I fear are all Big Brother's

- A reflection of our current situation where political correctness and cancel culture intersect. Youthful naivete confronts wisdom of old in today's changing world.

BLUE CHOICE

Didn't use your head
Another youth dead
Have you seen the news
Racial injustice, police abuse
Black man, white cop
Surely, you've seen this plot:

Black man, traffic stop
Guns going Pop! Pop! Pop!
The usual comes next
A lot of people vex
A video gone viral
Police force on trial

Why not de-escalate
Press "pause," recalibrate
No winners in this game
You're dead, or facing blame

Why does it continue then
We have all seen its end

Entire communities affected
When a life is not respected
Our actions often resonate
To a path of no escape
Walk away, take a breath
Your freedom, or his death

- Written after another police officer involved killing. This one, based on the video footage, could have been de-escalated and prevented.

COVID NIGHT THIEF

Like a thief in the night, it came
Unsure when, or who's to blame
A lethal assassin under a shrouded veil
A global specter of pandemic scale
Rich man, poor man, beggar man, thief
Weeping, wailing, and gnashing teeth
Doctors shell-shocked to disbelief
When will it all end, is there relief

Shutter the shops, close the borders
Mandatory "Shelter at Home" orders
Don the masks, gloves, and PPEs
Armor to combat a relentless disease
A cough, like a gunshot, clears a room
Hand sanitizer is the new perfume
"Sneeze and you die" is now trending
This Hitchcock saga, never ending

Our cities are toxic, thanks to a virus
Conspiracy theories, ubiquitous
No community, racial or ethnic
Escapes the reach of this pandemic

Royalty, Presidents, Prime Ministers
Laborers, policemen, janitors
Like all disasters, now and before
The ones affected are mostly the poor

The rich were vectors for this disease
Airborne droplets via cough and sneeze
Globally delivered via planes and ships
The rich for sure were on those trips
Poverty prevents the lower classes
Access to international travel passes
Unwittingly unleashed in diverse lands
Covid 19 now in the poor man's hands

History often likes to repeat itself
Repackaging disasters from its shelf
Black Plague, the infamous contagion
Wiped out half of Europe's population
Brought from Asia by merchant mariners
Afflicted mostly serfs and commoners
Pandemics seem to make the poor sicker
Conversely, it makes the rich much richer
Zuckerberg, Gates, Bezos, to name a few
While most suffered, their fortunes grew

Social distancing helped curb it's spread
Preventing many from ending up dead
It's easy for the rich to self-quarantine
Hunker in a space that's nice and clean
Estate homes and gated communities
Distancing the poor at all opportunities
Avoiding the underclass, is their norm
After so many years it's now an art form

These habits are foreign to the poor
Handed another disease with no cure
They who oft have nowhere to hide
Fare better outside the home than inside
Ten to a tiny shack, is not outlandish

That shack now becomes a petri dish
Comorbid conditions, health neglected
In close quarters, become those infected

Many have died, many more to come
Mainly our elders and years of wisdom
The economy is moving in fits and starts
Gun sales are galloping off the charts
People are uncertain about the future
Face of the new norm and subculture
Will we end like Babylon, perhaps Rome
Or like Mad Max Beyond Thunderdome

Peace and prosperity before the storm
Fear of contagion upset this calm
Panic and paranoia now common place
Masses retreating from the Rat Race
Executive orders keeping us home
Hospitalized patients dying alone
While body counts rocket to the sky
May the well of compassion never run dry

- This one speaks for itself. The idea was to highlight the vulnerability of the underclass to pandemics. When all is said and done, the poor are usually the biggest losers when any disaster strikes.

RIDDLE MI DIS

Riddle mi dis and riddle mi dat
Guess mi dis riddle and perhaps not
Born of the slums but moved uptown
Now the business turn upside down
Taken from the poor by landed gentry
Biggest rip off of twenty-first century
Corporate production is not a crime
The same for the Ras means jail time
Also, humiliation and police brutality
All for what nature gave to us free
They sacrificed their dignity, life, and limb
Perfected the art when pickings were slim
All a sudden food deh yah fi nyam
Nothing left for the sacrificial lamb
A bag of promises to calm the fools
Do this, do that, follow these rules
Colonial mentality at its bitter core
"Wha good fi di rich, nuh good fi poor"

Riddle mi dis riddle mi dat
Tell me what's in it for the Ras
Was a time when a Commercial Dread
An uptown singer, dreadlocked head
Not Rastafari or their philosophy
Cultural appropriation and hypocrisy
Never knew hardship nor sufferation
Now they run the whole operation
The hustling now moved to Wall Street
No food left for the Ras to eat
Tier 1, Tier 2, Tier 3
Amount you produce after paying the fee
Can't be a convict, do money laundering
International crimes, or drug trafficking
Tough restrictions by Official Decree
Even Bob Marley couldn't be a licensee
If you don't have money or foreign accent
Can't get a license from the government
Investors appearing on Jamaican TV
Some surprisingly don't sound like me
Were not from Africa or the diaspora
Can't speak pidgin, creole, or patois
They were "well-spoken and polite"
Quite a few also happened to be white
You have to have money to invest
Know how to profile and big up yu chest

Riddle mi dis, riddle mi dat
Should original Rastas get a shot
To obtain permits to cultivate
Their contribution we can't underrate
"It wi mad you" they said years ago
To the Ras and youths from the ghetto
Cured glaucoma, seizures, the flu
Modern science now proving this true
Opens the mind for spiritual meditation
They ordained it "Healing of the Nation"
Locally produced not foreign made

Comes as Bush and High Grade
Underground before legalization
Now poised for industrial exploitation
Projected windfalls all over the news
Sufferers still singing the blues
Sing along if this is getting you down
"Chase those greedy Baldheads out of......"

- When Jamaicans tell riddles, we always start with the phrase: "Riddle mi dis and riddle mi dat. Guess mi dis riddle and perhaps not." The poem is a riddle you must solve for yourself.

WHITE LIES

From the darkness, seen the light
This world is a better place
With a little color on your face
Especially if that color is white

White lies matter it's clear to see
If you're on the team
You are living the dream
In the land of the brave and the free

When they move into the 'hood
Whether rich or poor
With high credit score
The place supposedly changes for good

White lies matter it's clear to see
There's great self-esteem
On the winning team

In the land of the brave and the free

Ghettos are now "Economic Zones"
Designated by the President
To boost development
Now only the rich can afford to own

White lies matter it's clear to see
Not simple as it seems
Many plots, many schemes
In the land of the brave and the free

Was once called segregation
Now they bid you adieu
Then increase revenue
Renamed it gentrification.

White lies matter it's clear to see
To get on the team
You can't be Kareem
In the land of the brave and the free

Possessing unique characteristics
If they commit a crime
They'll do less time
According to the Bureau of Statistics

White lies matter it's clear to see
If you're not on the team
You're swimming upstream
In the land of the brave and the free

Who can incite a Capitol invasion
And get no blame
For igniting its flame
I'll give you a hint: (he's Caucasian)

White lies matter it's clear to see
They reign supreme

The creme de la cream
In the land of the brave and the free

So, it came as no surprise -
She embraced the Ukrainians
Then rebuked the Haitians
Perhaps Lady Liberty condones these lies

White lies matter it's clear to see
It's a recurring theme
Wink, wink - You know what I mean
In the land of the brave and the free

- Saw the impact of "gentrification" on Washington, DC on a recent visit to the city. The 'hood has been renovated and housing prices are off the charts. Many poor residents can no longer afford to live in the city. "Economic cleansing," is what I'll call it.

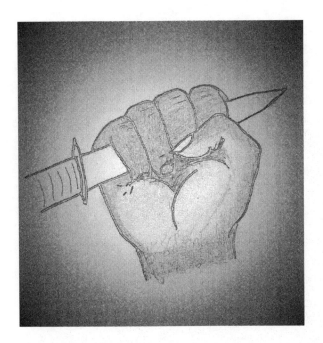

BLACK POWER

Seen it before, now I'm seeing it again
Same old promises, nothing in the end
Protests, riots, looting, the call to arms
Pundits, politicians sounding the alarms
Nothing will change, the same as before
Rich will stay rich, Blacks remain poor
Black Lives Matter, don't get me wrong
Just tired of hearing that played out song

The Black Power movement of the past
Got diluted by all the other outcasts
LGBT, Brown folks and Hispanics
Exposed our movement to be an old relic
They offered support, strength in numbers
Their agendas advanced, ours slumbered
A leader-less ship adrift in the doldrums
How did we get to this conundrum

All-in for a party where we have no voice
Ignored by the other as a matter of choice
Leaderless, powerless, its abundantly clear
Black Power now a sad state of affairs
Our agenda won't come via evolution
We must be willing to start a revolution
Nobody gives up power without a fight
Who will stand up and demand our rights

Black Lives must matter to us first of all
A house divided is destined to fall
Black on black crime is an epidemic
Even worse than a global pandemic
For violent crimes there's no vaccine
It's up to us to keep our house clean
A new social construct is what's needed
Where hope and prosperity can be seeded

Poverty, hopelessness, poor education
Root cause of crime in every nation
Revise laws, promote social intervention
Crime best addressed via prevention
Good education, nutrition - two big keys
Violence rare among those with degrees
United we become a large voting bloc
That's neither Republican nor Democrat
Politicians should compete for our vote
And institute policies that we can support

Accept ownership for what you do
An arrest is no time to practice judo
Shooting the innocent, there's no excuse
Neither subjection to physical abuse
Save all the drama for your day in court
Don't turn your arrest into a blood sport
In the Concrete Jungle there's no politics
Only "Judged by twelve or carried by six"

If you get beat up committing a crime

Did the crime......you know the rhyme
I won't be protesting on your behalf
My flag won't be flying at half-mast
Protesters may pillage their city center
It's their failing schools they should enter
Throw out their books, gut those schools
They're creating generations of literate fools
Greatest threat to the black population
It's not the Police, but poor education

Music producers stop promoting Black crime
Blaxploitation music is way past its time
Recurring theme in every gangsta rap song:
It's only the niggas you can "buss a cap" on
You can't "buss a cap" on a White, or a cop
This devaluation of Black lives has got to stop
They'll never "buss" it on a Jew, Asian, or Gay
They would be canceled that very same day
Apologies would follow as sponsors scatter
The same for us if Black lives really do matter

Make your child's education a priority
It is their gateway to opportunity
Slaves risked their lives just to learn
Our children shouldn't waste their turn
During slavery, those who were White
Feared slaves who could read and write
'Twas an open secret on the plantation
The educated Negro is a liberated man

Police stopping crime has been a disaster
We gave them a basket to carry water
More Police, more jails, longer sentences
Criminals don't muse over consequences
Death penalty has been around for years
Yet still long queues to the electric chairs
If the Death penalty can't deter crime
Then new approaches we have to find

Politicians use the police as scapegoats
To pacify the masses and claim our votes
Police work is relative to place and time
Becoming involved mostly after a crime
Police don't make laws, policies, or jails
We typically call them when all else fails
If their Second Amendment gets used
The Fifth Commandment could be abused

It is our community that's under attack
We must be the ones who clean up our act
High time to start respecting our brothers
Treat your sisters like we do our mothers
Don't call a brother "Dog," or sisters "Bitches"
Stop that talk about "stitches for snitches"
Love all the children like they're our own
Black Power and Respect begins at home

- An assessment of the Black Power Movement in the United States, highlighting the need to include personal responsibility as part of empowering ourselves.

WORD POWER

On the world stage, bigger and bigger
Ready to launch, finger on the trigger
There is a flaw and it's not hard to figure:
To stop him in his tracks... call him a nigger

What is this word that has so much power
Leads some to fight, make others cower
Slave logs first used it for classification:
A negro slave from Africa, sub-Saharan

Later used for racial abuse, subjugation
The victims, of course, the Black population
Many centuries of slavery kept us behind
Emancipation left chains on our minds

Niggers survived, thrived during slavery
Persevered, endured an atrocious history
400 years of terror, humiliation, pain
United in the struggle, we say "never again "

No word should have that power over us

Big up Malcolm, Harriet, Martin, Marcus
That the word is offensive, most will agree
Becomes hurtful only if we allow it to be

Rappers say nigger in just about every song
If a white guy repeats it, why is that wrong
If the word is that offensive, ban it for all
Who's to say it shouldn't be a judgment call

I say we embrace the word, remove its sting
They say nigger, we think Black Queen or King
We know haters aren't saying it to be kind
Woke intelligence shouldn't make us blind

It may be difficult to accept this now
To get past the why and then on to how
If we undertake this selfless sacrifice
Future generations may not face this vice

Say I'm naïve, crazy, or whatever you like
The word nigger doesn't haunt my psyche
When we're unshackled from mental slavery
Only then we'll find liberty and truly be free

So, if you call me a nigger, I'll smile all day
We've endured worse, came a very long way
Proud of my history, a past I can't change
Call me a nigger, see something strange

Europe built empires off colonial slavery
From the likes of Jamaica, Barbados, Haiti
Slaves built the South and stuffed US banks
Built the White House, no sorry, no thanks

Words are merely vibrations of the wind
Self-respect and dignity come from within
Chattel slavery, officially over and done
Time to focus our attention on reparations

Nigger by its current demeaning definition
Keeps us in an inferior, impotent position
Devoid of inherent, fundamental powers
To demand that which is rightfully ours

- This poem was written to stimulate debate and give my perspective on a very emotional and controversial word. The word "nigger" has been used negatively for centuries, to inflict mental damage and perpetuate an inferiority complex. We can't control what others may say, we can only control what happens in our minds when we hear this word. If being a "nigger" means your ancestors have survived and thrived after years of brutality and slavery, then I proudly embrace that word. If others choose to weaponize this word against me, it will do me no harm. The word effectively becomes a "dud," without any power. I welcome a world where all such words become powerless duds.

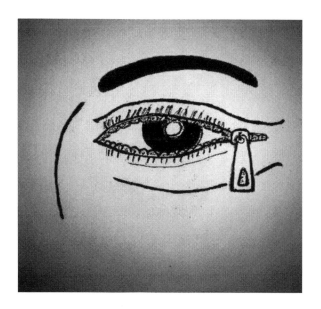

VICTIM EYES

Our world today is hypersensitized
With many people feeling ostracized
Hearts like fresh wounds exposed to air
Their badge of honor for all to stare
Even wind or falling rain will elicit cries
Alas! Finally! They are victimized!

Victim: a person harmed, injured, or killed
You can be one even if no blood is spilled
There's unwanted sorrow, pain, and shame
Which a few will embellish for its fame

A perceived slight, or an offending joke
Body language under the microscope
Those and more become something bigger
In the mind of a victim with a quick trigger

Some love being victims for the attention
There's empathy, you're worthy of mention

No need to "suck it up" or try to be brave
You got the attention that you've craved

There is implied power in victimhood
Only they can forgive, make things good
An apology to them is like a step back
To a face in the crowd, one in a pack
The spotlight fades, the crowd retreats
Silence ricochets from empty seats

We're in the middle of a culture war
So many things to get "victimized" for
With rules made up along the way
And those of old being no good today

Sticks and stones don't hurt as much
As offending words or an innocent touch
No need for dialogue to soothe outrage
Gets more views on a social media page

Forgive and forget is way too "old-school"
A fragile generation has changed that rule
When it's "eye for an eye, tooth for a tooth "
The real victim might just be the truth

- Written after noticing the trend of people who eagerly embrace victimhood and are offended by almost everything. They are also afraid to use face to face dialogue for conflict resolution. To them, there is no such thing as an honest mistake. Their quest becomes one for attention and revenge, sometimes with blatant disregard for the truth.

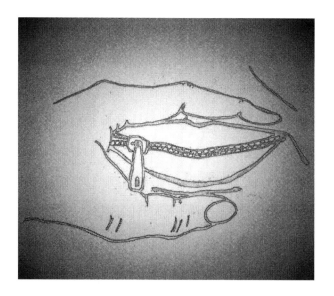

WHY CAN'T WE CHAT?

Wha dis, wha dat, we used to chat 'bout Sadat
Yitzhak Rabin and Yasser Arafat
Sanai Peninsula to Golan Heights
The Arabs, Palestinians, and Israelites

Wha dis, wha dat, today we can't chat
About Zionism, nakba, or even Hamas
Oslo Agreements you cannot mention
War crimes nor Geneva Convention

Wha dis, wha dat, Ivy League Sacred Cows
On bended knees, forced to do kowtows
Free speech and ideas they once inspired
Promote that now and they will get fired

Wha dis, wha dat, not another intifada
Israel won't hesitate to bulldoze Gaza
For atrocities of the October attack
Gaza Strip you might never get back

Wha dis, wha dat, how would it feel

If someone used you as a human shield
Cast into a battle of "slash and burn"
Where collateral damage is of no concern

Wha dis, wha dat, who lowered the bar
Is this the new standard now for war
Bombing your enemy beyond defeat
No chat 'bout surrender or retreat

Wha dis wha dat, we've seen this before
Body count so high the world can't ignore
Eye for an eye previously settled a score
Now it's 20:1 and will likely be more

Wha dis, wha dat, tell me who's to blame
When both sides file a victims claim
Should "might" decide which side is right
Do my questions make me an antisemite

Wha dis, Wha dat, I better stop chat
Before I get canceled right here on the spot

- Questions about the Israel/Hamas war in Gaza, and its impact on free speech and cancel culture.
- When Jamaicans encounter an unexplained mess they will ask rhetorically "Wha dis, Wha dat," meaning what is this, what is that.

ALL LIVES MATTER

I'm no saint, wasn't born in manger
Migrated to the US as a teenager
To systemic racism a total stranger
Didn't realize my life was in danger
Saw a cop standing on a black body
Posing and smiling, it was his trophy
From the police, the prisons, to the courts
Hunting a Negro is a lucrative sport

All lives matter, our rights are equal
Written into law to make it legal
All lives matter, none more than others
We must be the keepers of our brothers

Laws enacted, protect the status quo
Some on the books from centuries ago
Separated the races, especially the slaves
Separation extending down to the graves
Slaves got nothing from Emancipation
(Said slave considered three fifths a man)
Freed to be homeless and unemployed

A freedom, to date, most haven't enjoyed

All lives matter, our rights are equal
Shouldn't need laws to be official
All lives matter, none more than others
We must be the keepers of our brothers

Anger and rage as another brother die
Amid empty promises, bare-faced lies
Time to rebel, express the outrage
Emerge from bondage in that glass cage
Even Mother Nature vents her frustration
Quelling her wrath via volcanic eruption
Nature's laws are no different from man's
All actions have equal, opposite reactions

All lives matter, our rights are equal
Shouldn't need laws to be official
All lives matter, none more than others
We must be the keepers of our brothers

A life extinguished, a movement ignited
A country divided, needs to be united
This country struggling to be color blind
Saw the most diversity on the protest line
Unified chants of "No justice, no peace!"
Restraint and respect from the police
Equality and justice must be for all
A house divided is destined to fall

All lives matter, our rights are equal
Written into law to make it legal
All lives matter, none more than others
We must be the keepers of our brothers

- Inspired during the Black Lives Matter protests, 2020. The protests were spawned after a spate of police killings, of mostly unarmed, black males.

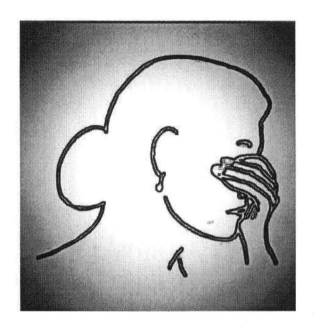

MOTHER'S REPRIEVE

Sit down, keep still
Relax and chill
Tune to the rhythm
Of optimism
Change beckoning
Ideas reckoning
Different styles
Being reconciled

Breathe in, breathe out
Listen, close mouth
Less ebb, more flow
Evolve and grow
Here, everywhere
No need for fear
Its Change ringing
Not the fat lady singing

- Written for all the mothers who grapple with the transformation of their children from child to adult. As we cede parental control, a comforting reminder that these changes represent normal, human, social evolution, and do not spell the end of the world.

QUESTIONS

A simple question, answer me please
Why does Jamaica have so many Chinese
Not the born and grow from days back
The just land with suitcase and backpack
"Nihau," hello, my Chinese greeting
They smiled and replied in Mandarin
Came years ago, as indentured servants
Now here as contractors and merchants
No official word on the exact number
Governments seem "Dumb and dumber"

Chinese, among the hardest workers alive
They can land in any country and thrive
Have a formula they use everywhere
Shop, live on top, and family work there
Another thing that should also be clear
Absolutely no local can be their cashier

Came for construction and settled here
To the average Jamaican is that fair
Are Chinese taking jobs away from us
Are they working here with legal status

Is it how Americans feel when we arrive
In their country, on our success drive
Or why native Blacks in South Africa
Brainwashed by Mr Xena and Ms Phobia
Commit those unforgivable atrocities
Against Africans from other countries
Are foreign workers to be ostracized
Should they first become naturalized
A government statement would be nice
To calm the sufferers raising their voice

Do they have visas or residency permits
Why is their presence this open secret
Jamaica for Jamaicans, my gut says
But exactly who is a Jamaican anyways
Foreign born, expatriates the world over
The people who make up our diaspora
If you're abroad, do you lose your space
How about local born, but foreign based
The patois, accent, and birth certificate
Is that what makes you legitimate

Jamaicans are Africans, Jews, Arabs, Asians
Europeans, Hispanics, and Americans
Many more I'll refer to as "others"
Legally Jamaicans and our brothers
The Chinese have a visible presence
Increasing in numbers and influence
Many ethnicities make our nation village
Am I just suffering from "white privilege"
Is our motto still "Out of many one…"
Somebody please answer mi question!

- Written after a 2018 visit to Kingston, Jamaica. On my flight to Kingston, I noticed about thirty Chinese nationals heading to Jamaica. Never seen those numbers before, especially going to Kingston. This, coupled with the increased presence of Chinese nationals in Jamaica, led me to ask some questions.

COUNTRY ESSAYS

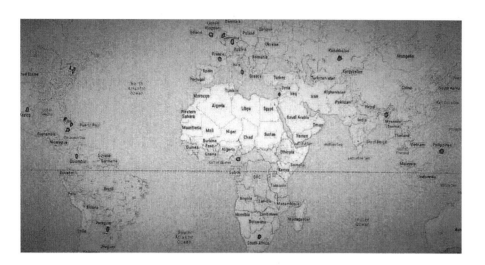

Map of the world with black dots identifying the countries that I have drafted essays about.

To pass the time during long flights from some of the countries I visited, I would write notes on the things that stood out about that country, its people, and my experience. Below is a collection of essays, written in prose, on some of the countries I have visited.

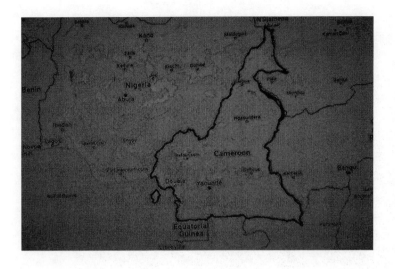

WHITE MAN!

Mi black maybe brown
Mi brown yes mi black
Didn't have a clue
It came outta the blue
Like a sniper attack
White man! White man!

Pickney come from far
Pickney from near
Rushing the car
Like mi ah big star
When all mi could hear
White man! White man!

Right pon the equator
Cameroon, Africa
The same ancestor
The same creator
As me from Jamaica
White man! White man!

All round is black skin
Jam pack melanin
So pickney nuh care
Dem chat weh dem hear
Without thinking
White man! White man!

There, if you nuh black
You must be white
Cause only ting brown
Is dirt pon the ground
Must be mi eyesight
White man! White man!

Live in the US
Where mi always black
Took a long flight
All a sudden mi white
Can't wait to get back
White man! White man!

- Written to commemorate the lasting, fond memories of my visits to Cameroon, West Africa. All the kids in the rural villages referred to me instinctively, as "white man." It was like I was from another planet. "Pickney" is the patois word for child/children.

ISRAEL

Flew to Tel Aviv the old Israeli capital
Under tight security via airline El Al
Got interrogated by their operative
"What's our plan, where will we live?"
Will be volunteering at a Dental Clinic
Going there to help, no need to panic
Tel Aviv is artsy and set by the sea
Think of rush hour in New York City
Drove from Tel Aviv to Jerusalem
Got to the apartment about 9pm
It was cold, had one space heater
Not enough if you're from Jamaica
Went to bed late that first night
And woke up to the brightest daylight
Buildings are made of Jerusalem stone
Makes the whole city look white as bone

Dental Volunteers Inc. clinic day one
Met with the coordinator Mrs. Sharon

Dentists Valter and Jacob, Sima assistant
Made our time there quite pleasant
Clinic ended daily at one pm
Then it was off to tour Jerusalem
The old city is divided into sections
Each representing different religions
The Western Wall is a Jewish rite
Dome of the Rock, important Islamic site
Church of Holy Sepulcher, worthy of awe
The tomb of Jesus is its main draw
Crowds are thick in this solemn room
I got road raged kneeling at Jesus' tomb

Old City, New City, soldiers everywhere
Def con delta in full combat gear
Fingers on triggers, hammers cocked
I pray that they don't stumble or drop
The City is tense, nobody laughs
Not soldiers, pedestrians, or retail staff
No smoking signs were there to ignore
Employees smoking in their own store
Smoking was a common, evident truth
Like Eve, Adam, and the forbidden fruit
It comes back to bite them in the end
Will tragically cast them out of Eden

People were friendly don't get me wrong
But it was love with a dose of suspicion
Shabbat is sacred, few cars on the street
Need to go somewhere, use your feet
The city is still alive in Muslim areas
Except during their regular prayers
Jerusalem has many religious sects
Orthodox Jews are a visible subset
The hat, tassels and two curly locks
A dead giveaway that they're Orthodox
Western Wall tour, no foul no harm
Our tour guide wore a heavy sidearm
A somber history told with Jewish pride

Armed security brought us back outside

Bethlehem was a whole 'nother story
Important place in Christian history
Church of Nativity, Christ's birthplace
Is in the West Bank, a cluttered space
No Jews, it seems, are welcomed there
The road signs make that quite clear
The West Bank is mostly Palestinian
Not officially recognized as a nation
Though things there may seem cool
They are not happy under Israeli rule
While they ponder the Jewish downfall
They must deal with their border wall
The West Bank and the Gaza Strip
Are front lines of Jewish-Arab conflict

To Teddy Stadium for a soccer game
Home team supporters were insane
Beiter Jerusalem in yellow and black
Thwarted Maccabi Netanya's attack
Hardcore fans, the "LA Familia" squad
Don't want Beiter to recruit any Arab
Since its founding, according to them
None has played for Beiter Jerusalem
One-one at the end, the score was tied
Took us all on a roller-coaster ride
The Dead Sea is 450m below sea level
Rock salt on the floor just like gravel
To enter its water please wear shoes
Spare your feet from a pointed abuse

This is Israel, country of David's star
Arabs and Jews in a virtual war
Today a bombing, next day a stabbing
No reprieve from the enemy within
Some say it's fueled by a religious core
Many have died, there'll likely be more
Eye for an eye makes no one secure

When each side wants to up the score
Jews, Palestinians, their "Promised Land "
Is situated in the same, exact location
Promises, it's said, comfort only fools
Unless they're the ones making the rules
Many will be called; the chosen are few
Will they speak Arabic, and/or Hebrew?

Salam, shalom, toda rabah, shukran
Blessings from two neutral Jamaicans

- A reflection on our trip to Israel. My sister Karen and I traveled to Israel, December 2018, to do volunteer work at a clinic serving Jews and Arabs.
- The territorial borders of Israel are in dispute, so no attempt was made to highlight its border on the map.

PARAGUAY

Paraguay, Paraguay the Latin brother
(Different father, same mother)
To a Caribbean island named Jamaica
It's a land locked island in South America
"Run with it," "no problem," they make do
Sounds ironic, but it works for those two
Paraguay is lined by rivers circumferentially
And quite underdeveloped economically
A virtual island in the true sense of the word
In world development, their status is third
Looks out of place in South America
Would be more at home next to Jamaica

Bordered by Argentina, Bolivia, and Brazil
Their economies grew, Paraguay's stood still
Years of war didn't grant him any favors
From his opponents and hostile neighbors
Six million the population – not very large
They could all fit inside Brazil's garage
The Guarani are the people, language, and culture
It's seen on the currency and their architecture
Five thousand guranies to one US is fair

And makes this guy an instant millionaire

The people are friendly and unpretentious
Went out of their way to accommodate us
Beef is a staple, there are no apologies
Guarani and Spanish, the official languages
Soccer's their game, it's played everywhere
And when they play, always a crowd there
Zoning is confusing in capital Asuncion
See shack beside auto repair, beside mansion
Four on a motorcycle, no need to stare
Donkey carts on the roads are also not rare
No speed cameras, and stop lights are few
Potholes and speed bumps appear out the blue

Bus stops are hard to find in Asuncion
You stand on the corner and wave your hand
The bus may stop....... or it may not
IF it doesn't, you try again on the next block.
Public buses are old and dilapidated
Their insides are frugal and uncomplicated
They rattle, shake and race down narrow streets
You get on, sit down, and lock your butt cheeks
Drivers take fares, give change, check payload
Once in a while, they'll even look at the road
I have a theory, though just a guess
They wear blindfolds for the driver's test!

Copa Libertadores Feminina is why we came
To pay homage to "The Beautiful Game"
Dogs and cats were seen in the stadium
Who said humans alone are to have fun
Our Chiny Asher played for Santa Fe
Colombian posse, let me hear you say yeah!
Santa Fe didn't make it out the first round
As a result, we're homeward bound
We say goodbye, hasta luego
To Paraguay, Jamaica's hermano

- As champions of Colombia, Independiente Santa Fe went on to compete in the Copa Libertadores Feminina, that year in Paraguay. We were there to support my daughter, Chiny. The country and its level of development reminded us of Jamaica.

KAZAKHSTAN

Left from Dulles, Washington
Destination Shymkent, Kazakhstan
The first stop is in Astana
South of the Russian border
To the southeast via Almaty
Most populated Kazakh city
Heading to the home of Kazygurt BIIK
In the former Soviet Republic

Vast reserves of natural gas
Perfect place for Chiny Ash
Took the "silk road " across the land
Like Marco Polo and Genghis Khan
Off to Shymkent, further west
Nothing but dirt, a desert at best
Leader Narsultan Nazarbayev
Longest serving Kazakh Prez

Nine hours ahead, the sun is set
Absorbing it all with a deep breath
Previat, caczilla, dobre dien
Hi, hello, can't say what I mean
Team is nice, facilities cozy

English ok, my Russian's lousy
Will wake to face another day
Champions League football, Thursday

Three forty tenges to one dollar, US
A happy Dads, no need to guess
Official languages: Kazakh and Russian
There's Kazakhs, Russians, Uzbeks, Koreans
From Tartar, Iran, Germany, Uzbekistan
Culturally diverse, indeed cosmopolitan
Won't forget my roots or my culture
Big Respect to my posse from Jamaica!

- Out of the blue, Chiny got an invitation to play for a team from Kazakhstan, which was trying to qualify for the Champions League. Reluctantly, she accepted the offer and joined the team in Ireland for the qualifying games. The team, Biik Kazygurt, made it all the way to the round of sixteen, of the Champions League. I made a visit to Kazakhstan during Chiny's time there.

COLOMBIA

Made my way to Colombia
Staying in the capital, Bogota
With over eight million personas
Fifth largest city in the Americas
May twentieth is the birthday
Of my third daughter Chiny A
That I was there, she didn't realize
Planned with Yenny, a big surprise
Hugs, kisses, and a big smile
Precious moment for father and child
Professional soccer she came to play
Her team, Indipendiente Santa Fe

Outside the city, it's nice and green
Muy tranquillo, very serene
Bogota is a compost of brick and mortar
Nothing green, nothing to water
Graffiti as an art form is everywhere
Even in majestic Simon Bolivar Square
The city is all hustle, bustle, and people
Cars, motor bikes, roller skates, bicycles
Rushing to somewhere in all directions
The lowest and the slow, the pedestrians

Caught in the middle of a medieval court
Where crossing the road is a blood sport

Crime is high, but you wouldn't know
Unless you turn on the TV, or the radio
A church was held up while in session
Patrons robbed of worldly possessions
Justice was swift as justice should be
The Lord's robbery was caught on CCTV
There were petty crimes, murders, a house bombing
Grills, bars, barbed wires that said, "Don't come in!"
Santario Monserrate, church in the mountains high
Though afar from the city it's still fortified
Trust in the Lord, but cover your bases
So, armed security in strategic places

El Campin, the stadium of Santa Fe
Is where rivals Millionarios play
Their games sometimes get out of hand
Police in riot gear, dressed like Iron Man
Downtown comes alive after dark
With entertainers, artists, and harbor sharks
On the weekends church and Fiestas are a way of life
A sanctuary, I suppose, from their nine to five
My time is up, I have to go
Adios Bogota! Hasta luego!

- Against my recommendations, Chiny and her friend, Yenny, accepted invitations to play for Independiente Santa Fe in the inaugural women's professional football league in Colombia. I took a trip there, a couple months prior to the playoffs, to help Chiny get back up to speed, and into the first team. She was having a difficult time adjusting to the altitude and, like Yenny, was coming off an injury. Independiente Santa Fe went on to become the first champion of La Liga Feminina Profesional de Futbol Colombiano. Chiny was instrumental in that Championship run.

SOUTH AFRICA

The plane land, yes the plane land
Airline that we flew was South African
The country is clearly one of extremes
From mud huts to estate housing schemes
From Johannesburg on to Soweto
Modern European changes to ghetto

Went to Cape Town with a game plan
Learn as much as we possibly can
Roll with the penguins in Boulder
Hike Cape Point, Africa's south border
Cape of Good Hope, westward further
Touring with Maya and Raksha.
Learned some things we never knew
The sand is white and the sea blue
The first Europeans to pass through,
Vasco da Gama and Bartholomew
Table Mountain seen on the horizon
Robben Island was Mandela's prison

Fly off to safari in Durban
Heart of Zulu tribe and nation

Shaka Zulu big in the area
Legendary chief, great warrior
Now on the wildlife reservation
Looking at animals and vegetation
Got stuck in the mud by the river
On the highway of the predators
Just stayed calm and kept my cool
From the city, but I was no fool
Used my experience with snow
In no time we're back on the go
Saw rhino, giraffe, zebra
Nayala, cheetah, impala
Lion, warthog, and some hippos
We didn't see any mosquitos

Leaving South Africa tomorrow
Bitter-sweet with joy and sorrow
Going home to my family
Lord, what a beautiful country!

- South Africa is a beautiful country with something for everyone: wildlife, scenery, mountains, beaches, rivers, etc. It is also a country of extremes: first-world opulence to abject poverty; mud huts to mansions and crime and corruption.

HOLLAND

It has a population of 17 million
The densest in the European Union
The Kingdom of the Netherlands
Is officially what's called Holland
Being its most influential province
It's been called Holland ever since
The name Dutch was by association
To neighbor Germany, aka Deutschland
Universiteit Utrecht is why I came
To review rhinoplasty and up my game
Used to seeing cars, buses, and trains
Discovered bicycles roaming untamed

Though it has quite a few people
There are less of them than bicycles
Dedicated lanes, no hills to surprise
Makes Holland a bicyclist paradise
Boys, girls, mom, dad, grandma
All star in Holland's bicycle drama
Three on a bicycle not worth a stare
Bike riding sometimes a family affair
To cycle in US, a helmet you'll require
The Dutch view that as surplus attire
Bicycles are ubiquitous creatures here
On the roads it's "pedestrians beware!"

Red light, green light, ready set go
Here's comes a herd of iron Buffaloes
Wild beasts on the Dutch Serengeti
Emulating Formula 1's, Mario Andretti
Some zipping fast, some laboring slow
With luggage racks and wheelbarrows
Headphones on, cell phones in hand
Drifting along with reckless abandon
Bicycles at midnight, say it's not so
Someone must be landing a UFO
Bells ringing, lights seen, then unseen
I think I'm having a bicycle dream

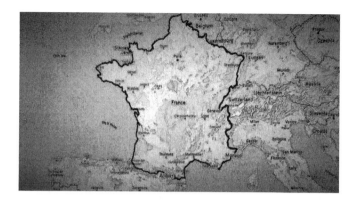

FRANCE

From Utrecht to Amsterdam to Lyon
Women's World Cup in France was on
Met up with siblings while over there
Keith, Karen, Jackie, and nephew Shakir
Also, daughters Imani and Mponya too
Youngest Gigi came in from Saskatoon
Son, Daniel, was also in the fam zone
Bringing good vibes and testosterone
To Grenoble, to see the Reggae Girlz
Competing with the best in the world

Brazil against Jamaica at Stade de Alps
Sadly, the Brazilians took our scalp
Three to zero, not the best we could do
Daughter, Chiny Asher, made her debut
That I was proud, don't bother to ask
In that euphoria I continue to bask
Over seventeen thousand tickets sold
Just about all the stadium could hold
Most waving the black, gold, and green
Of our country, my daughter, our team

Next, to Nice, heading due south
Sea and sunshine are what it's about
A South Beach flavor in a foreign land

Shores caressed by the Mediterranean
Monaco to the east is relatively near
One in three residents is a millionaire
The rich, famous and their exotic cars
Is what this Principality is known for
To Reims, just northeast of "Paree"
Known in France as Coronation City
To play Italy, the soccer powerhouse
Wasn't David v Goliath, but lion v mouse
Gave it their all, put up a decent fight
Experienced Italy exposed a neophyte
The score was five to zero in their favor
A bitter taste for all Jamaica to savor
Australia next week, then we're done
Closing the books on an exciting run

To capital Paris, for a mini vacation
Mostly to be one with inner vegetation
I speak no French this should be clear
I'm calling things as to me they appear
Paris seems old, worse for the wear
(Why are immigrants still coming here)
The homeless are mostly foreign origin
You can tell by accents and color of skin
Tiny restaurant on every street corner
Seats are outside to make them larger

Bright colors are an anomaly here
Unless it's the yellow resistance wear
Those bright colors are the "yellow vests"
Garments of anti-government protests
It's shades of blue, grey, mostly black
Nobody smiles or makes eye contact
Eiffel Tower, Arc de Triumph, don't forget
The Bastille, and Madam Marie Antionette
No Louvre, Versailles, avoided the crowd
Louis XIV's palace, made him so proud
Electric scooters were quite a nuisance
I feared them most in Paris, France

185

The streets are crowded without them
Them on sidewalks is a huge problem
Heading home via Reykjavik's island
Au revoir France, gooan daginn Iceland

- Written after a two-week trip to Europe to coincide with the 2019 FIFA Women's World Cup. I started off by attending a rhinoplasty course in Utrecht, Holland, before heading to France. There I met up with the rest of my family to watch my daughter, Chinyelu Asher, and the Jamaican national soccer team compete in the World Cup finals.

ITALY

A trip to Rome, Eternal City of dreams
Once an empire that reigned supreme
Leonardo Da Vinci, the airport's name
Italian genius of Renaissance fame
There a random stranger grabbed my bag
Didn't show an ID, or wear a name tag
His request was rejected, I told him FU!
Then armed soldiers appeared out the blue
'Twas an undercover cop, I now deduced
Passport and bag made sense to produce
No apologies, reason why, or explanation
They seemed in no mood for conversation
European countries, directly, or by intent
Don't welcome those of African descent

Spent the first few days exploring Rome
Sistine Chapel, it's world-famous dome
Coliseum, Pantheon, Fountain Tevi
World's smallest country in Vatican City
Rome's population is three million
In rush hour traffic I counted each one
Via car we're off to the mountains cool
Son Daniel to attend a Perugian school
It's a city of stones and fortified walls

There to learn the language, play football
Didn't like the vibes, so we pulled him out
Made the right decision, there's no doubt
Today he's a Boarded Family Physician
Still plays football, only for recreation

Roma v Fiorentina at Stadio Olympico
A missed flight meant that we could go
Scalpers at the stadium selling biglietti
To see Luca Toni against Francesco Totti
A battalion of Soldiers met us there
In helmets, shields, and combat gear
Was this a football, or a war game
Here, I guess, they're one and the same
Stadium was crowded with vocal fans
The Ultras shouting offensive slogans
Flares flung on the field, but no problem
Firemen at the ready, to remove them
Didn't stop the game, no time for that
Roma continued to launch their attack
"El Capitano," the legendary Totti
Scored a goal, made home fans happy
One-zero it ended to cheers and jeers
Hard-core Ultras still waving their flares
Tomorrow we're off, homeward bound
Back to work, once back on the ground
To Italy we say a grand "arrivederci!"
Extinguished our flame in the Eternal City

- Italy, a beautiful country, and an important locale for European history. A great place for European history buffs to visit.

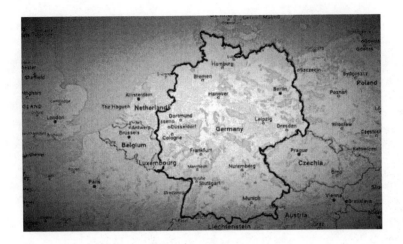

GERMANY

The land of VW, BMW, Benz, Porsche
Eight hours later I'm in Dusseldorf
From the airport to Bochum, via train
'Twas like clockwork, couldn't complain
Bochum University for microvascular
Weeks of studies and extracurricular
The city is clean, orderly to a fault
They cross roads only when it says "walk"
Jaywalking is rare, looks out of place
Penalties and fines you may have to face

University is orderly, continues the trend
Course participants, a diverse blend:
Germans, English, Dutch, Nigerians,
Brazilians, French, Taiwanese, Indians
Weekends were free, do as we please
Train travel in Europe is such a breeze
Trip to Amsterdam for a scenery change
Prostitution is legal, also Mary Jane
Smoke filled air, prostitutes on display
Didn't partake in either, I'm proud to say
A canal cruise and a historical tour
Needless to say, I'm quite the bore

By train to Dortmund for my next trip
Borussia Dortmund v Bayern Munich
Fantastic game, zero-zero the score
Loud, cheering fans and beer galore
Crowded Restrooms, as they should be
I Joined the masses for a roadside pee
By train to Bochum, it was toes to heels
I now know exactly how a Sardine feels
Relieved to be back at Bochum hotel
I plan a trip to visit my cousin Nigel

Hamburg, German city of superlatives
The hometown of my German relatives
The second most populated German city
Home of Uncle Luddy, Nigel and family
Right on the river Elbe to the North Sea
The largest shipping port in Germany
Bochum to Hamburg, a scenic train ride
Included some personal drama inside
One hour away from my destination
I was subjected to police interrogation
"Open your suitcase, show identification!"
Did as they asked without hesitation
Turned out OK, things didn't head south
But left a really bitter taste in my mouth

Cousin Nigel was a very obliging host
Well accomplished, but not one to boast
Great guitarist, headlines his own band
Performs at varied venues European
His band opened Airbus' headquarters
And, for me, that was just the starters
Got backstage passes to the Lion King
That two Jamaicans were starring in
A tour of the city gave some perspective
Hamburg's cultural, commercial objective
Back to Dusseldorf, then off to USA
No reason to extend my German stay

Danced to its beat, listened to its tune
Don't think I'll be back anytime soon

- A summary of my first and only visit to Germany for a microvascular surgery course in 2018.

CUBA

Where Gulf, Caribbean, and Atlantic meet
La Republica de Cuba takes her seat
To her west is Mexico, Haiti to the east
Bahamas, Turks, and Caicos within reach
Due north is the sunshine state, Florida
90 miles to the south you'll find Jamaica

1492 Columbus reached Cuba's shores
Spain would rule for 400 years more
A Slave led economy is how Spain ruled
Way past when Slavery was no longer cool
Slavery abolished there in 1882
Sugar cane and tobacco earned revenue

Ceded to US post Spanish-American War
President McKinley then its defacto Tsar
1902 Cuba got its independence
Though never could shake the US' presence
The US occupies Cuba to this day
Ask any Cuban about Guantanamo Bay

Post-independent Cuba's economy grew

The one's benefitting were the rich few
In 1959 Cuba became a different venue
Batista's regime Che and Fidel overthrew
A communist country from then till now
How they survived, I still don't know how
Economic blockades and counter coups
Cuba always seems to get negative news

We visited Cuba in 2001
Part of an official Jamaican delegation
Jamaica's Medical Association was invited
Cuba's Ministry of Health was delighted
To share best practices and philosophies
Health care in urban and rural communities
Hospitals we visited gave official tours
Community clinics opened their doors
World class standards is what we did see
Health care for Cubans is absolutely free

To some in our group 'twas a deja vu trip
Were past recipients of Cuban scholarships
My sister, Karen, brother-in-law Devon
Graduates of one such Cuban institution
Their colleagues of old embraced us there
Santa Clara we went to welcoming cheers
Streets well paved, didn't see many potholes
Neat and tidy sidewalks, a sight to behold

Hermana, a classmate, and close friend
Took us round Cuba, showed us the trend
Horse drawn buggies our transport d'jour
Horses had baggies to catch their manure
Stayed with her family, ate Cuban food
Housing was sparse, but nothing crude
Bought rations, even shopped with pesos
Hung out with her family and the amigos
Cigars were a must; Cubans are the best
Though I don't smoke, I didn't protest

Cubans were proud, loved their country
Many served overseas with the military
Most Cubans I met liked Fidel Castro
Blamed all problems on the US embargo
Major dissenters left via the "Boat lift"
Presented Castro with a presidential gift
Prisons were emptied, homosexuals sent
Thousands to Miami, by boats they went

My safety in Cuba was never a bother
Everywhere in Havana, a police officer
Children at midnight playing in the streets
My sign of safety and a delightful treat
Fancy hotels, beyond most Cuban's reach
Especially on the coast at Veradaro Beach

White sand shores, sea crystal clear
We rushed its waters without any fear
Was it the sea or just a very large pool?
If not for the salt, many it would fool
Went to a party couldn't mambo or salsa
Didn't try Danzon, official dance of Cuba

Cuba's President for life was Fidel Castro
Che Guevara, another Revolutionary hero
"History will absolve me," Fidel often said
That verdict's still out, his epithet been read
Cuba presents an ethical question for me
What would one sacrifice for one's liberty?

- Visited a beautiful country, rich in culture with proud, resilient people. Account of the boat lift as told by Brigadistas who studied in Cuba.

SWEDEN

No Covid test needed, nor health report
I'm free to travel to Arlanda Airport
In Sweden we land, its capital Stockholm
Land of Volvo and my old Eriksson phone

The Kingdom of Sweden, as it is known
Fifth largest country in the Euro-zone
Norway is west and north, Finland is east
Denmark is south, Baltic Sea is her beach

10.5 million is the population
87% of which live in areas urban
This is 1.5% of the country's land mass
The rest is forests, lakes, trees, and grass

Famed for Vikings, great warriors of history
A Great Power of Europe till the 18th century
Launched many wars against its neighbors
Russia, at times, being foe and enabler

Defeated by Russia in Peter the Great's reign
Marking the end of their European campaign
Now 200 years of peace Sweden has seen
Celebrated with a ceremony in 2014

Mostly neutral in war, always seeking peace
The Ukrainian invasion is causing unease
NATO membership grant to Sweden please
Bound to catch a cold if Russia should sneeze!

Travelled to Sweden to visit my daughter
Bring some warmth and exchange laughter
She went to Sweden, soccer to play
For the Damallsvenskan team AIK

Saw their first game in cold and snow
It was AIK against KIF Orebro
Played on AIK's field at Skittleholm
Where they kicked butt, then sent KIF home

'Twas winter and there was nothing to do
Sight-seeing options were relatively few
To the Viking museum on one such trip
Still in awe of that massive Viking ship

Read their stories of triumph and conquest
Viking were clearly amongst the world's best
Brave and valiant warriors to admire
Once occupied half of Holy Roman Empire

Downtown Stockholm where the King resides
No fence or wall to keep visitors outside
One armed guard at the door's entrance
What if an idiot decides to take a chance?

Seven-Eleven store on every other block
In Stockholm they are the number one shop
Didn't go north enough to see Northern Lights

Aurora Borealis is such a phenomenal sight

Education and health care in Sweden are free
Swedes only, no visitors, migrants, or refugees
Many homeless people living on sidewalks
Their "great" social system - is this just talk!

King Gustaf heads a constitutional monarchy
Power lies with Parliamentary Democracy
Its Riksdag makes laws, rules, issue decrees
King only there to smile and say "cheese"

World's 12th highest per capita income is true
But in Sweden you pay taxes out your wazoo!
Businesses, workers, goods, transportation
Every transaction is taxed, even fornication

Swedes excel in every industry it seems
Reaching heights most only see in dreams
Ingmar Bergman's movies are entertaining
Bjorn Borg, their tennis star was amazing

ABBA the pop group; very popular and rich
Also world famous is Zlatan Ibrahimovic
Greta Thunberg the teen climate activist
The Nobel guy, Alfred, also makes the list

Sweden has over 200,000 islands
The country has more than any other one
Such a number I find very hard to believe
(Who made that count, and was it a Swede?)

Cash in Sweden unlike non-grata personas
'Twas hard to get rid of my Swedish kronas
Electronic transactions are what's preferred
show them cash, they might flip you the bird

People were nice, though somewhat formal
On the streets - no smile, no hello is their normal

English is understood by everyone there
Meatballs and potatoes, a common fare

The Swedes are huge, even women are tall
My extra-large equates to their small
Leaving Sweden now, feeling like a gnome
Think I'm developing Stockholm syndrome

- Visited Sweden during winter when not much happens outdoors for me. Didn't get to see much of the country.

ENGLAND

Hip, hip hooray we land in UK
24th March, on a Saturday
Took London tube to the hotel
Off to sleep like we're under a spell
Tour London, the tourist trap
Sight-seeing first, then off to shop
Double decker bus with open top
Froze our butts as temperature dropped
Windsor Castle, changing of the guard
Westminster Abbey, Scotland Yard
London Bridge, Big Ben, Tower London
River Thames and Palace Buckingham

Next day to St Georges Hospital
Me and Imani, delegates official
Head and Neck Dissection Review
Learn some things we never knew
From thought leaders and experts
Ten-hour days, a whole lotta work
Many had called, the chosen few
Imani and Dads did get through

To Manchester on the Virgin train
Check out the city, took in a game
Only saw rain, we didn't see snow
Occasional sun, but no rainbow
Saw Man U via hospitality ticket
Defended our home, and our wicket
Man U two, Swansea zero
Alex Sanchez the game hero

Met cousin Julie and family once
Olympian daughter won the bronze
Julie made dinner, food was great
Ate everything, nearly licked the plate
Met my other niece, Celine (not Dion)
From Hamburg, studying in London
Great musician and a budding star
Gave her a classic Gibson guitar

Back to the airport, heading home
No more in London shall we roam
Had to work the very next day
Jet lag we had to keep at bay
Thank God flight wasn't delayed
If we miss work, we don't get paid

- Written on our way back from the UK. My daughter, Imani, and I, traveled to London, England to attend a surgical course, and to meet some of our relatives living in England.

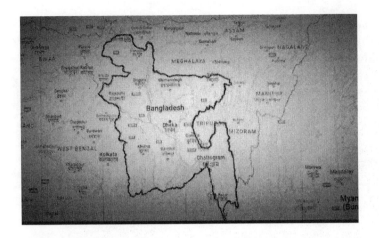

BANGLADESH

Out of the ordinary, new, and Fresh
Went on a mission to Bangladesh
165 million the population
Eight most populous of all nations
Separated from India after Partition
Originally known as East Pakistan
Pakistani alliance didn't last long
Declared independence 1971
A Low-lying country, lush and green
Largest river delta mankind has seen
Land of the Bengals, tigers call it home
Sundarbans mangroves they freely roam

Surgeons for Smiles the name of our team
Repair cleft lips and restore self esteem
The lead surgeon and SFS President
Ed Zebovitz, my former Chief Resident
We arrived in the morning in Capital Dhaka
One hundred miles to the west is Kolkata
India's Bengali capital, near the Ganges
Same language spoken as Bangladeshis
From Dhaka to Savar we traveled by van
To a hospital specializing in rehabilitation
Center for the Rehab of the Paralyzed

A safe community to those often despised
"Service to suffers is service to God" they say
A mission statement they proudly display
A poignant reminder of what is at stake
Guides our actions and decisions we make

The Rehab Center is a gated community
What they emphasize is self sufficiency
There's a hospital, schools, dorms, shops
Vegetable gardens to grow their own crops
Armed soldiers meet you at the front gate
Its on-site mosque will keep you awake
Five times a day, a loud sermon to hear
Midnight sermons were too much to bear
8 am to 8 pm in the hospital we toiled
A surgery machine that was very well oiled
Nurses, doctors, and supporting staff
All tirelessly working on our behalf
Instruments, rooms, meals - no problem
If any develop, they'll quickly solve them
Many kids we treated, too much to count
Measured quality of care, not the amount

Playing fields and courts also onsite
Children having fun, much to our delight
Saw the most intense basketball game
Sidelines packed, seemed everyone came
Players battled for ball, also positions
Wheelchairs overturned by heavy collisions
Gave it their all and then even more
Three to two was the game's final score
Applause and cheers for the winning team
Went all out, accomplished their dream
They're not disabled, just differently abled
Defying the odds, and how they're labeled
On the trip home there's time to reflect
On the Center's mission worthy of respect
Back in the land of the brave and the free
Humbled by our experience at the CRP

- Surgeons for Smiles led an amazing mission to Bangladesh, performing cleft lip/palate repairs at the CRH. We were all inspired by the mission of the hospital and the dedication and commitment of the staff and residents.

PHILIPPINES

Zebovitz, Pham, Asher the OS troupe
Recruited from the US by The Bicol Group
Zebovitz - team leader, me an understudy
A role in this mission for every able body
Oral surgeons, general surgeons, OBGYNs
Anesthesiologists, nurses, other stand-ins
Masbate, Philippines, final destination
There for volunteer work, not a vacation

BWI to Detroit, then off to the Orient
Twenty-four hours later, a new continent
Looked cold, patchy snow on the ground
Nagoya, Japan is where we touched down
Onward southwest, off to the Philippines
White sand beaches, and waters pristine
An Archipelago in Southeastern Asia
Neighboring China, Vietnam, and Malaysia
Over 7000 islands make up this nation
One hundred nine million, their population
Named to honor King Philip II of Spain
Colonized in 1565, during his reign
A colony for over three hundred years
Spain left a legacy which still perseveres

Spanish surnames are quite the norm
Christianity, religion to which they conform

Ceded to US post Spanish-American War
This Asian outpost then ruled from afar
Invaded by Japan during World War II
War's end meant independence anew

Capital, Manila, where we landed at night
Manila to Masbate meant another flight
Manila is congested, nobody is on time
Has "big city" problems, especially crime
"Death for drugs" signs posted everywhere
Zero tolerance makes this warning sincere

Masbate to the south is mostly rural
Farms and rice paddies are not unusual
By jeepney to hospital for a quick tour
Back in the morrow for surgeries galore
Cleft lip and palate, a big problem here
An ugly defect that makes others stare
Children are shunned, kept out of school
Parents are blamed, often ridiculed
Surgery, the chance to make things right
We'll be screening patients past midnight

Masbate's Governor welcomed us there
His security detail gave us the scare
Forty-eight soldiers armed to the teeth
SUVs, motorcycles, a gun-mounted jeep
He must be precious, or he's really hated
Either way, his security wasn't debated

"Magandan Umaga" means good morning
Another busy day for surgery is dawning
Sun-up till sunset and way past after
Surgery filled days, packed with laughter
Patient transport gurneys are nonexistent
Post-surgery transport by nurse or parent

Two-foot gurney is what they are dubbed
Surgery to postop with a whole lot of love
Emergency Epinephrine, expired and black
Who would care if having a heart attack
Everything is recycled, disposables kept
Washed and packed overnight as we slept
Only one night nurse to care for the pack
Parents and families picked up the slack
There they were sleeping under the beds
On cardboard and mats resting their heads
Many miles away, from whence they came
There for their kids without any shame

After two long weeks it's time to stop
Round up the team, lock up our shop
Our mission was over, 'twas time to go
A patient started bleeding; pressure low
Rushed to the OR as an emergency case
Our departure imminent, no time to waste
Internal bleeding suspected post-op
Made sense to tackle this as a co-op
I'll get instruments, you prepare the site
The patient was literally turning white
Site prep was slow, in concentric circles
Seen faster preps done by old turtles
"Scalpel!" she yelled. "Need to be quick!"
If any infection, give an antibiotic
Surgery successful, thanks to Ed's wife
We left Masbate without losing a life
Back to Manila, then to the US we'll fly
"Paalam" we say, the Filipino goodbye

- Participated in a few medical missions to the Philippines in early 2000s. On our first mission to the city of Masbate, the chief medical officer outlined the number of cases performed by the previous team, highlighting the number of fatalities. The theme for our mission was "No Fatalities," which we were proud to fulfill.

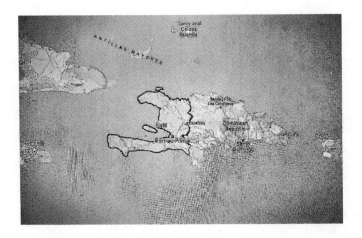

HAITI

Ferdinand and Isabella, rulers of Spain
Sponsored Columbus during their reign
Find a trade route to India via the sea
And claim any new lands for His Majesty

India to the east, had an overland route
A very dangerous and expensive commute
Mongols and bandits on the way there
For the most part it was "buyers beware!"

The science of navigation and astronomy
Re-examined the earth and its geography
The earth is not flat, it is a large sphere
Sail West, and East will eventually appear

Unknown land masses, fuzzy calculations
Created uncertainty for earth's navigation
Was an opportunity a King couldn't refuse
For a few maravedis, was little to lose

Spain provided men; the ships were three
The Pinta, The Nina, The Santa Marie (a)
Ferdinand freed prisoners to man the ships

Murderers and robbers made those trips

The journey was longer than was estimated
The criminal crew becoming quite agitated
This voyage, to them, seemed like a waste
Mutiny, Columbus was about to face

After five long weeks, they saw in the air
Birds, the sign to sailors, that land is near
Bahamas they sighted in 1492
Swore they found India, Columbus' crew

Natives they saw they called Indians
Thinking they had arrived in Asian lands
Hispaniola was the first settled for Spain
The start of Europe's long Caribbean reign

Thus began a legacy worthy of shame
Murder of natives in Christianity's name
Hispaniola's west was seized by France
A hostile take-over, with scant resistance

Saint Domingue, it was called there after
A French colony built on slave labor
Sugarcane and coffee were the cash crops
With the brutality of slavery as the backdrop

The worst of atrocities done to mankind
While church and state chose to be blind
Sugar, back then, valuable as oil today
Gunboat diplomacy, the order of the day
Pirates of all nationalities gathered there
Likes of Black Beard, Morgan the Buccaneer

Saint Domingue the prized colony of France
Providing goods and riches in abundance
More valuable than Louisiana, at a glance
An idea of Saint Domingue's importance
Now the poorest country in the hemisphere

Very interesting how they wound up there

Renamed Haiti in 1804
After a rebellion led by Toussaint L'Ouverture
The only ever successful slave rebellion
Defeating the powerful French battalion

The war in Haiti, France needed to finance
Louisiana sold to US for a mere pittance
For Haiti, France fought tooth and nail
Guile and bravery made the slaves prevail
Napoleon's army, then Europe's mightiest
Three times in Haiti, they were second best

To correct history and rewrite its books
One follows facts, and not how things look
Should then be clear to all, as it is to me
Before Waterloo, Napoleon met his Haiti

Word of this, other Islands couldn't know
Haiti then subjected to a trade embargo
The colonial powers became deathly afraid
United to impose an international blockade

Whites in Haiti then systematically erased
By boat to Louisiana, white survivors raced
The embargo sank Haiti into poverty
Ever since, there's been no recovery

Poverty and politics have ruled Haiti's fate
Hindered by a location atop tectonic plates
Every time they shimmer, rattle, or shake
Haiti subjected to one more earthquake

Set in the middle of the hurricane corridor
Disasters knock regularly on Haiti's door
Floods, landslides, earthquakes, hurricanes
Contribute to the country's growing pains

Years of mismanagement and corruption
Crippling debts, like the French restitution
Coups, counter-coupes, foreign invasions
Political instability, brain drain migrations

Jean Jacques Dessalines, Henry Christophe
Boyer, Faustin, not to mention, Papa Doc
The Duvaliers and their Tontons Macoutes
Stifled generations of Haitian youths

A nation of well over 11 million
Largest in the Caribbean, by population
The most mountainous, and botanical
Port-au-Prince is the country's capital

Poorest in the region, there is no contest
Problems of Haiti akin to an ant's nest
Layered, twisted, and branched like a tree
Fixing Haiti, "it's like plowing the sea!"

Volunteered in Haiti with a medical team
Right after the earthquake, 'twas a dream
More like a nightmare, to be specific
Port-au-Prince looking post-apocalyptic

Via a church loaned jet to Port-au-Prince
Pastors and clerics we had to convince
Medical personnel on the flights to allow
Doctors and nurses needed right now
Faith and salvation to be put on pause
Sacrificed their seats for a noble cause

All aboard were medics except one celebrity
Won-G bought fuel for our flight to Haiti
Runways overcrowded, nowhere to land
A scenario for which no one had planned

Two hours we circled airport Louverture
Our pilot took us on a Haitian aerial tour

The time over Haiti allowed observation
Country has a problem of deforestation
Finally, we landed, it was past midnight
Slept on the tarmac till day became light

Foreign soldiers encamped at the airport
To the US contingent, they all had to report
Only the UN and US could bear weapons
No other soldiers could carry any guns

At the airport it seemed we would be stuck
UN soldiers to the rescue with a dump truck
Off to the hospital to set up our shop
The scenario we saw made our jaws drop

Jam-packed all over the hospital's grounds
Hundreds of flimsy tents there to be found
There were families of four, five and six
In tents of twig poles covered by plastic

Over 200,000 deaths, the injured more
So many I think, they stopped keeping score
Lack of food, no utilities, social troubles
Multiple communities reduced to rubbles

House atop house, built on shaky ground
No surprise then when it all tumbled down
Masses in the city gathered in protest
No food or jobs the source of the unrest

Criminal gangs rule the streets at night
Scared the fight out of my "fight or flight"
Port-au-Prince is unsafe, that is for sure
A city armed soldiers are afraid to explore
Saw UN soldiers cower in their beds
Afraid of the Zombies, the living dead

Surgeries every day, around the clock
Feelings of guilt whenever we stopped

Patients everywhere, on benches and floors
Many more outside beating on the doors

All types of injuries, mostly broken bones
From earthquake, concrete, falling stones
A week we stayed, had hoped to do more
Loved the people, their spirit, the folklore

Left Haiti via US Military cargo plane
US citizens only, all others had to remain
Like cattle, we're packed in the cargo bay
A somber end to an eye-opening foray

- The history of Haiti is a classic example of exploitation, discrimination, and the crippling impact of an economic blockade. Exploited during slavery and later via the French Restitution; Discriminated against today. The country has never recovered from the economic blockade imposed by European powers after winning independence.

MEXICO

Ho, ho off we go
All the way to Mexico
To Monterrey in Nuevo Leon
Two flights, Customs, immigration
Hotel Cityexpress outside the city
With Karen, Devon, Raksha, Njeri
Concacaf Championship, why we came
Another World Cup berth is our aim
Our Reggae Girl, Chiny, we came cheer
Black, gold, and green is what we wear

Cambio Dinero the first thing we do
Twenty pesos for a dollar, is this true
Cost of living so low, I'm spending less
Monterrey the city ex-pats love best
Five dollars for a meal that feeds four
Obesity in Mexico, need I say more
The subway system, efficient and cheap
Easy to travel like one of the peeps
City seemed safe, no crime to report
Amigos simpaticos, offered support

213

Monterrey, capital of Nuevo Leon state
An industrial city with varied landscape
Mexico's second largest by population
Mexico City we know is "el "number one
Two teams from Monterrey in Liga Mex
Monterrey Rayados and UNAL Tigres
Went to their games to sold out crowds
Tigres' fans, more spirited and loud

Concacaf women's qualifier teams
Usual suspects there, so it seems
Mexico, Jamaica, USA, Canada
Haiti, Trinidad, Costa Rica, Panama
Mexico to the semis was a sure bet
An apple cart Jamaica about to upset
Hopes of the home team ended in shame
The Mexican women didn't win a game

The Reggae Girlz had a modest ideal
A World Cup berth they wanted to seal
First Mexico, then Haiti, and it's done
Beat the US, and we'll be number one
Haiti was dispatched without questions
The US, however, are World Champions
Five-nothing the score, it was obscene
Team USA scoring like a well-oiled machine

Made it to the semis against Canada
Lost to the country from North America
Costa Rica the team we next had to face
A battle to claim coveted third place
Chance after chance, the Girlz left it late
A lone goal it took to seal their fate
Jamaica prevailed in second overtime
From a Van Zanten goal, oh so sublime
History was made and it took a little luck
The Girlz qualified for a second World Cup

Tournament over, we'll close this book
Girlz finishing with a positive outlook
Third in a region dominated by the US
Canada always among the world's best
Much to ponder as we leave Monterrey
The US and Canada are not far away
Jamaica, with more time and finances
Next year in Australia, I'll fancy our chances

- Visited Monterrey, Mexico to witness the Jamaica national senior women's football team qualify for a historic second Women's World Cup Finals.

CRY BELOVED JAMAICA

Jamaica, beloved Jamaica
Land of wood and water
Fertile soil, lush and green
White sand beaches, mountains serene
So much food we don't die of hunger
Different story with rape and murder
Kingston to Mobay, country wide
Reputed gangster, innocent child
None too old or even too young
If blood haffi run, it ah go run!

Jamaica, beloved Jamaica
Revered and loved the world over
Marley, Bolt, Garvey, Lowe
Impossible is a word we don't know
Guns, Lotto scam, extortion, cocaine
Crime and violence spoiling our name
Out of control, mostly senseless
Urban to rural, very ruthless

Jamaica, my beloved island
Two countries, rolled into one
One for tourists and rich people
One for ghetto pickney, and all evil

Sky's the limit for the first one
Other in a glass cage, less than a man
Island paradise, flowing streams
Not everything here is as it seems
Police, layman, even thief
Keep one eye open when they sleep

Jamaica, beloved country
Awfully nice place to be
Crime and corruption we have to fight
So we can leave doors open at night
Painful sacrifices must be made
Tune's been called, Piper to be paid
It won't be easy, the journey long
Out of many we must remain one
Tourist resort or Special Crime Zone
It's our country, ah fi wi own!

- Written on my way back from Jamaica, one year before the General Elections that would see the Jamaica Labour Party return to power. The JLP's promise of reducing crime was their campaign theme. It was made in response to the deadly crime wave that was gripping the island.

EPILOGUE

September twenty eighth 11:59, (Too much space between the lines)
We place a period
Eagerly anticipating starting a new line...
September twenty-nine
For one,
A new page of life has begun
A new chapter bright
Promising of joy, adventure, and fun
A new day standing firm on all the lessons learned
A new chance for debt to be repaid
For the universe to give this one what they've earned
This day, more special than all the rest
Thankfully, I praise God for giving me the sheer best
A Father? A man?
Titles do not do
For in a league all his own, he is uncontested by all the rest.
On this new day that has dawned
Because you paved the ground for us to run our best in life's marathon
For being second to the Man upstairs for whom we can call upon
For never failing to be the one we can always depend on
I wish the Happiest of Birthdays to you
The one and only
Original Don.

Mponya Asher

Made in the USA
Columbia, SC
23 February 2025

54200834R00124